AF559986

DISASTER MANAGEMENT

DISASTER MANAGEMENT

Editor

Dr. Rabi Narayana Misra

DISCOVERY PUBLISHING HOUSE PVT. LTD.

INDIA

Published by:

Namit Wasan

DISCOVERY PUBLISHING HOUSE PVT. LTD.
4383/4B, Ansari Road, Darya Ganj
New Delhi-110 002 (India)
Phone : +91-11-23279245; 23253475; 43596065
E-mail : discoverybooksindia@gmail.com
discoverypublishinghouse@gmail.com
namitwasan9@gmail.com
web : www.discoverypublishinggroup.com

***First Edition:* 2019**

ISBN: 978-93-88854-04-7

Disaster Management

Printed at:
Infinity Imaging Systems
Delhi

Preface

Disaster management aims to reduce, or avoid the potential losses from hazards and to provide appropriate assistance for active and effective recovery. The disaster management is an ongoing process, the Govt. and the society has to plan to reduce disasters.

It is an unpredictable event which happens instantly without no time, further it affect a large number of people disrupting normal life and leading to large scale devastation in terms of loss of life and property. Further after disaster the social-economic condition will seriously effect for a larger time. Disaster may be natural like flood, earthquakes, Environmental like industrial accidents, forests fires, etc., complex emergencies include conflict situations and war, pandemic emergencies involving a sudden onset and create serious health problems. It also affects economic and social disorders.

This book is very much helpful to all students of science, Govt., planners, engineers, scholars, industrialist and general public at large.

Dr. R.N. Misra

Acknowledgement

I am very thankful to all paper contributors of this book. It is no possible in my part to edit this book without their help and cooperation.

I convey my thanks to all lions club Gold members specially to Dr. B.M. Sasmal, Dr R.N. Padhy Sharma and Smt. Swarnaprava Misra for their kind co-operation. I also extend my thanks to outside delegates like Dr. D. Tata Roa, Principal. Dr. G. Chandraya, Principal and others. I also thankful to Smt. Swarnaprava Misra my wife for her active co-operation to publish this book.

I extend my heartful thanks to Mr. Tilak Wasan, the owner of Discovery Publishing House Pvt. Ltd., New Delhi for his co-operation to publish the book without any hesitation. I also thankful to Mr. Namit Wasan was an and his team of members to take active part to publish the book in time.

Dr. Rabi Narayana Misra

Contents

Disaster Management **Pages 1-16**
Edited by: **Dr. Rabi Narayana Misra**
ISBN: 978-93-88854-04-7
Edition: **2019**
Published by: **Discovery Publishing House Pvt. Ltd., New Delhi (India)**

Chapter 1 Disaster Management in India

[1]Dr. Santosh Kumar Badatya

Introduction

India is considered as the world's most disaster prone country. Like many other countries in this region, India is plagued by various kinds of natural disasters every year, such as floods, drought, earthquakes, cyclones and landslides. Millions of people are affected every year and the economic losses caused by natural disasters amount to a major share of the Gross National Product (GNP). Natural Disasters are huge economic burdens on developing economies such as India. Every year, huge amount of resources are mobilized for rescue, relief and rehabilitation works following natural disaster occurrences. **Disaster management** (or emergency **management)** is the creation of plans through which communities reduce vulnerability to hazards and cope with **disasters. Disaster management** does not avert or eliminate the threats; instead, it focuses on creating plans to decrease the effect **of disasters.**

The *United Nations defines a disaster* as a serious disruption of the functioning of a community or a society. Disasters involve wide spread human, material, economic or environmental impacts, which exceed the ability of the affected community or society to cope using its own resources. There is no country that is immune from disaster, though vulnerability to disaster varies. There are four main types of disaster. These are Natural disasters: Environmental emergencies, Complex emergencies & Pandemic emergencies.

---

[1]Dr. Badatya, Asst. Prof. in Finance MBA, Dept. of SMIT, Berhampur.

More recently, several institutions with a focused mandate on disaster management have come up in various parts of the country. The Ministry of Home Affairs (Disaster Management Division), National Institute for Disaster Management (New Delhi), Gujarat State Disaster Management Authority (GSDMA), Orissa State Disaster Management Authority (OSDMA), Disaster Mitigation Institute (Ahmedabad) can be seen as initiatives taken in the right direction. Local, regional, national and international organizations are all involved in mounting a humanitarian response to disasters. Each will have a prepared disaster management plan. These plans cover prevention, preparedness, relief and recovery.

Types of Disasters

There is no country that is immune from disaster, though vulnerability to disaster varies. There are four main types of disaster:

- *Natural disasters:* including floods, hurricanes, earthquakes and volcano eruptions that have immediate impacts on human health and secondary impacts causing further death and suffering from (for example) floods, landslides, fires, tsunamis.
- *Environmental emergencies:* including technological or industrial accidents, usually involving the production, use or transportation of hazardous material, and occur where these materials are produced, used or transported, and forest fires caused by humans.
- *Complex emergencies:* involving a break-down of authority, looting and attacks on strategic install at Environmental emergencies ions, including conflict situations and war.
- *Pandemic emergencies:* involving a sudden onset of contagious disease that affects health, disrupts services and businesses, brings economic and social costs. Any disaster can interrupt essential services, such as health care, electricity, water, sewage/garbage removal, transportation and communications. The interruption can seriously affect the health, social and economic networks of local communities and countries. Disasters

have a major and long-lasting impact on people long after the immediate effect has been mitigated. Poorly planned relief activities can have a significant negative impact not only on the disaster victims but also on donors and relief agencies. So it is important that physical therapists join established programmes rather than attempting individual efforts.

Plan for Disaster Management

Local, regional, national and international organizations are all involved in mounting a humanitarian response to disasters. Each will have a prepared disaster management plan. These plans cover prevention, preparedness, relief and recovery.

- **Disaster prevention**

These are activities designed to provide permanent protection from disasters. Not all disasters, particularly natural disasters, can be prevented, but the risk of loss of life and injury can be mitigated with good evacuation plans, environmental planning and design standards. In January 2005, 168 Governments adopted a 10-year global plan for natural disaster risk reduction called the Hyogo Framework. It offers guiding principles, priorities for action, and practical means for achieving disaster resilience for vulnerable communities.

- **Disaster preparedness**

These activities are designed to minimize loss of life and damage - for example by removing people and property from a threatened location and by facilitating timely and effective rescue, relief and rehabilitation. Preparedness is the main way of reducing the impact of disasters. Community-based preparedness and management should be a high priority in physical therapy practice management.

- **Disaster relief**

This is a coordinated multi-agency response to reduce the impact of a disaster and its long-term results. Relief activities include rescue, relocation, providing food and water, preventing disease and disability, repairing vital services such as telecommunications and transport, providing temporary shelter and emergency health care.

- **Disaster recovery**

Once emergency needs have been met and the initial crisis is over, the people affected and the communities that support them are still vulnerable. Recovery activities include rebuilding infrastructure, health care and rehabilitation. These should blend with development activities, such as building human resources for health and developing policies and practices to avoid similar situations in future.

Disaster management is linked with sustainable development, particularly in relation to vulnerable people such as those with disabilities, elderly people, children and other marginalized groups. *Health Volunteers Overseas publications* address some of the common misunderstandings about disaster management. Disasters and their management generally get discussed in their aftermath but practically it should result in planning and preparing the strategy to tackle and mitigate disasters in a responsible and effective manner. Disasters, both natural and unnatural, are macro level events or processes, which induce disturbances and turmoil for a prolonged life-threatening environment for a community.

World Development Report (IFRCRC, 2001 categorizes natural disasters into hydro meteorological (earthquakes, cycolcanic eruptions, etc.) and geophysical (landslides, droughts, etc.) categories. The scope of unnatural disasters broadly encompasses conflicts, civil strife, riots and industrial disasters. In the past decade (1991-2000), natural disasters have killed 66,59,598 people, accounting for 88 per cent of all due to disasters. Similarly, unnatural disasters have killed 86,923 people during the decade. Nearly two-thirds of the people killed in these disasters hail from developing countries like India, with only four percent of the casualties being reported from highly developed countries (IFRCRC, 2001).

Disaster management is essentially a dynamic process. It comprises the classical management functions of planning, organizing, staffing, leading and controlling. It also involves many organizations, which must work together to prevent, mitigate, prepare for, respond to and recover from the effects of disaster. Disaster management would therefore include immediate response, recovery, prevention, mitigation, preparedness and .....the cycle goes on. India is considered as the world's most disaster prone country. Like many other countries in this region, India is plagued by various kinds of natural disasters every year, such as floods, drought, earthquakes, cyclones and landslides. Millions of people are affected every year and the economic losses caused by natural disasters amount to a major share of the Gross National Product (GNP).Natural Disasters are huge economic burdens on developing economies such as India.

Every year, huge amount of resources are mobilized for rescue, relief and rehabilitation works following natural disaster occurrences. In India, a closer analysis of what transforms a natural event into a human and economic disaster reveals that the fundamental problems of development that the country faces are the very same problems that contribute to its vulnerability to the catastrophic effects of natural hazards. The principal causes of vulnerability include rapid and uncontrolled urbanization, persistence of widespread urban and rural poverty, degradation of the environment resulting from the mismanagement of natural resources, inefficient public policies, and lagging (and misguided) investments in infrastructure. Development and disaster-related policies have largely focused on emergency response, leaving a serious under-investment in natural hazard prevention and mitigation.

Conventional Response to Disasters

Humans have managed disasters and an overview of our past experiences shows that management of disasters is not a new concept. For example, in ancient India, droughts were effectively managed through conventional water conservation methods, which are still in use in certain parts of the country - like Rajasthan. Local communities have devised indigenous safety mechanisms and drought-oriented farming methods in many parts of the country.

The subject of disaster management is not mentioned in any of the three lists in the Seventh Schedule of the Indian constitution, where subjects under the Central and State governments are specified. In the post-independent India, a journey through the five-year plans points to the fact that the understanding of disasters was to mitigate droughts and floods; schemes such as the Drought Prone Area Program (DPAP), Desert Development Program (DDP), National Watershed Development Project for Rain fed Areas (NWDPRA) and Integrated Water Development Project (IWDP) are examples of this conventional paradigm *(Planning Commission, 2002).*

Recent Changes

The late 1990s and the early part of this century marked a watershed in Disaster Management in India. The Orissa Super Cyclone and the Gujarat Earthquake taught the nation a hard lesson. The experiences of the stakeholders like the state, voluntary sector and the communities at large helped in initiating the planning process pertaining to preparedness and mitigation of disasters.

A welcome step in this direction was setting up of a High Powered Committee on Disaster Management in 1999, which submitted its report in 2001. An important recommendation of the committee was that at least 10 per cent of plan funds at the national, state and district levels be earmarked and apportioned for schemes that specifically address areas such as prevention, reduction, preparedness and mitigation of disasters. Also for the first time in the planning history of India, planners devoted a separate chapter titled *'Disaster Management: The development perspective'* in the tenth five-year plan document (Planning Commission, 2002).

More recently, several institutions with a focused mandate on disaster management have come up in various parts of the country. The Ministry of Home Affairs (Disaster Management Division), National Institute for Disaster Management (New Delhi), Gujarat State Disaster Management Authority (GSDMA), Orissa State Disaster Management Authority (OSDMA), Disaster Mitigation Institute (Ahmedabad) can be seen as initiatives taken in the right direction.

There has also been a concerted effort on the part of the state to mainstream Disaster Mitigation initiatives in Rural Development schemes. One of its example is the coordination between the Ministry of Rural Development and the Ministry of Home Affairs, which is now the nodal ministry for coordination of relief and response and overall natural disaster management, for changing the guidelines of schemes such as Indira Awas Yojna (IAY) and Sampoorn Grameen Rojgar Yojna (SGRY) so that the houses constructed under IAY or school buildings/community buildings onstructed under SGRY are earthquake/cyclone/flood resistant.

Role of NGOs

Since the community is the first responder in any disaster situation, there is a great need for community level initiatives in managing disasters. The initiatives taken by various agencies, including the state, need to be people-centric and the level of community participation should be gauged through the role played by the community in the process of planning and decision-making. Efforts should also be made to strengthen local economies, thereby making people independent of external assistance. The voluntary sector has been in the forefront of mobilizing communities, enabling them to cope with disasters in the past decades. Their initiatives and experiences have been consolidated and demonstrated on a larger scale with the help of the state. Development organizations working in communities share a good rapport with the community, which helps the state in implementing its plans more effectively; village level plans prepared after the Super Cyclone in Orissa could be seen as an example of the same.

The focus of any disaster management plan now incorporates the following:

- Community Based Disaster Preparedness.
- Development of block, Gram Panchayat and Village disaster management plans.

This has been made possible through continuous advocacy by development organizations like Action Aid, Oxfam, CARE-

India, etc. These initiatives have been scaled up by the state, which has taken efforts to integrate disaster management plans with the larger developmental plans at all levels such as Village/Panchayat/Block/District/State.

Government has got the whole machinery in place and the relief work is carried out with the help of the following agencies- Indian Red Cross Society, Indian Institute of Tropical Meteorology, UNDP India, Tata Energy Research Institute, Housing and Urban Development Corporation Ltd., Ministry of Urban Development and Council for Advancement of People's Action and Rural Technology (CAPART). All these agencies in the past responded to major disasters in the country. For example, in the state of Orissa in the aftermath of Super Cyclone in 1999, they provided immediate relief services to the affected families. Further, they collected and distributed relief material, helped in providing immediate shelter, supported voluntary organizations for implementing activities pertaining to the relief and rehabilitation work and provided training to masons for repairing damaged houses. The vast network of partner voluntary organizations provides the Government with a greater opportunity to implement Disaster Management plans at the grassroots level much more effectively.

Challenges for the Future

There is a growing need to look at disasters from a development perspective. Disasters can have devastating effect on communities and can significantly set back development efforts to a great extent. But then, it could also offer an opportunity to invest in development efforts in a post disaster scenario. Disasters are opportunities for communities to reinvent themselves. Disaster prevention, mitigation, preparedness and relief are four elements, which contribute to and gain from the implementation of sustainable development policies. These elements, along with environmental protection and sustainable development, are closely inter-related. The Yokohama Strategy, emanating from the international decade for natural disaster reduction in May 1994, emphasizes that disaster prevention, mitigation and preparedness are better than disaster-response in achieving the goals and objectives of vulnerability reduction.

The Government of India has adopted mitigation and prevention as essential components of its development strategy. The Tenth Five Year Plan emphasizes the fact that development cannot be sustainable without mitigation being built into the development process. In brief, Disaster Management is being institutionalized into development planning. But, there are various underlying problems in the whole process. In fact, a number of problems stem from social inequities.

In the long run, the onus is upon the local communities to handle disasters with the help of the state and other such organizations. It is a well-known fact that the community dynamics is quite complex in a country like India. There is a need to address specific local needs of vulnerable communities through local traditions and cultures. Restoration of common property resources with the participation of the local level bodies is a real challenge. The historical focus of disaster management has been on relief and rehabilitation after the event but now the focus is on planning for disaster preparedness and mitigation. Given the high frequency with which one or other part of the country suffers due to disasters, mitigating the impact of disasters must be an integral component of our development planning. One of the glaring lacunae in the process of Disaster Management in India has been the overlooking of unnatural disasters. The recent efforts focus purely on natural disasters, whereas the current global situation also demands initiatives in managing the impact of unnatural disasters. Developments at the international level, particularly the civil wars and civil strife in Eastern Europe and Southern America culminating on 9/11 have brought the issue of unnatural disasters at the forefront of disaster management. The global community has recognized the serious consequences of Nuclear, Biological and Chemical (NBC) warfare. This remains a serious challenge for India to address in the near future.

The need of the hour is to chalk out a multi-pronged strategy for total disaster management comprising prevention, preparedness, response and recovery on the one hand and initiate development efforts aimed towards risk reduction and mitigation on the other. The countries in the Asia-Pacific region should establish a regional coordination mechanism for space-technology based disaster mitigation and strengthen co-operation, Luan suggested, adding that they also need to set up an all-weather and all-time comprehensive space-based disaster mitigation system and share the information. A pro-active stance to reduce the toll of disasters in the country requires a more comprehensive approach that comprises both pre-disaster risk reduction and post-disaster recovery. It is framed by new policies and institutional arrangements that support effective action. Such an approach should involve the following set of activities:

The Indian Scenario

The Indian sub-continent is highly vulnerable to cyclones, droughts, earthquakes and floods. Avalanches, forest fire and landslides occur frequently in the Himalayan region of northern India. Among the 35 total states/Union Territories in the country, 25 are disaster prone. On an average, about 50 million people in the country are affected by one or the other disaster every year, besides loss of property worth several million.

Table 1.1: Total Number of People Reported Killed and Affected by Disasters in India

Year	Total number of People reported killed	Total number of People reported affected (in person)
1986-1995	42,026	561,472,9952
1996-2005	85,001	686,724,143
2005	5,405	28,262,805

Source: World Disasters Report, 2006- Disaster Data.

In the 1970s and the 80s, droughts and famines were the biggest killers in India, the Situation stands altered today. It is probably a combination of factors like better resources management and food security measures that has greatly reduced the deaths caused by droughts and famines. Floods, high winds and earthquakes dominate (98%) the reported injuries, with ever increasing numbers in the last ten years. The period from 1973 to 2001 has been associated with a large number of earthquakes in Asia that have a relatively high injury- to death ratio. Floods, droughts, cyclones, earthquakes, landslides and avalanches are some of the major natural disasters that repeatedly and increasingly affect India. Table 1.1 depicts an annual damage due to Natural Disasters (for the year 1985-1997).

The natural disasters directly impact economies, agriculture, food security, water, sanitation, the environment and health each year. Therefore it is one of the single largest concerns for most of the developing nations. Different natural hazards cause varying levels of physical damage to *infrastructure* and *agriculture* with implications for their indirect and secondary impacts. Drought causes heavy Crop and Livestock losses over wide areas of land but typically leave infrastructure and productiv capacity largely unaffected. Floods and Cyclones cause extensive whereas damage to both infrastructure and agriculture, depending on their timing relative to the agricultural cycle. While Earthquakes have little impact on standing crops excluding localized losses but can cause wide spread devastation of infrastructure and other productive capacity over relatively large areas. India is hit by one major natural disaster or the other almost every year wherein the loss of life is accompanied by losses of the magnitude that is difficult to comprehend. The decade (1990-99), which was the **International Decade for Natural Disaster Reduction (1990-99),** it witnessed a spate of large-scale disasters that defied all attempts to stem them. These included the Latur (Maharashtra) Earthquake of 1993 killing about 10,000 persons, the Andhra Pradesh Cyclones of 1990 and 1996, killing about 1000 persons each, the Gujarat Cyclone of 1998 killing over 3,500 persons and the Orissa Super-Cyclone of 1999 killing about 10,000 persons. Besides these major events, there ere smaller earthquakes in Uttarkashi, Chamoli and Jabalpur, and frequent floods in the northeast, Uttar Pradesh, Bihar and Kerala. Unfortunately, these disasters were not taken up as learning opportunities, and lessons were not drawn from them to the extent to be prepared in combating future disasters. What happened in Gujarat in 2001 and the way it was handled are grim reminders of the fact that we still need to learn and improve much. The precise cost of the disaster in terms of loss of lives, property, loss of development opportunities, etc. cannot be clearly assessed, counted or scaled. The costs of disaster are clearly inequitable, falling heavily only on the few. Disasters result not only in loss of shelter but also create hardships, lack of food availability, temporary loss of livelihood and disrupt socio-economic activities. Some of the losses may be redeemable and compensated for through disaster relief and insurance. However, apart from economic dimension, such disturbances have their psychological and social dimensions as well, which need to be studied, and documented besides developing appropriate mitigation strategies.

THE HIGH POWERED COMMITTEE ON DISASTER MANAGEMENT

In August 1999, a High Powered Committee (HPC) on Disaster Management was set up at the behest of the Prime Minister to look into the issue of Disaster Management Planning at national, state and district levels. The Committee, under the chairmanship of Mr. J. C. Pant, had examined the issue of disasters holistically, considering both natural and man-made disasters. Emphasis is on preparedness, and the role of different stakeholders in this activity. The Committee has had a number of consultations with various groups, including academicians, technocrats and voluntary agencies to arrive at a common plan. The Committee submitted its report along with a National Response Plan (HPC Report, 2001). The HPC now stands converted into the Working Group of the national committee under the Prime Minister.

Due to the increasing frequency of natural and man-made disasters and their severe impact on the individuals, society, economy, natural resources and environment,

Government of India constituted a High Powered Committee (HPC) on Disaster Management in August 1999 to prepare comprehensive plans for National, State and District levels. The HPC has rightly stressed on the need for a comprehensive and holistic approach towards dealing with all kinds of disasters. From a compartmentalized response oriented approach, a coordinated, holistic and participatory approach has been recommendedl 1. HPC identified thirty one disasters in the country. These disasters have been categorized into five sub-groups depending on generic (origin) considerations and various departments/ministries dealing with various aspects. These five sub-groups are as follows:

1. Sub-Group I–Water and Climate Related Disasters

This sub-group includes Floods and Drainage Management, Cyclones, Tornadoes and Hurricanes, Hailstorm, Cloud Burst, Heat Wave and Cold Wave, Snow Avalanches, Droughts, Sea Erosion and Thunder and Lightning.

2. Sub-Group II–Geologically Related Disasters

It includes Landslides and Mudflows, Earthquakes, Dam Failures/ Dam Bursts and Mine Fires

3. Sub-Group III–Chemical, Industrial & Nuclear Related Disasters

In this category, the chemical and industrial and nuclear disasters have been included.

4. Sub-Group IV–Accident Related Disasters

Forest Fires, Urban Fires, Mines Flooding Oil Spill, Major Building Collapse, Serial Bomb Blasts, Festival Related Disasters, Electrical Disasters and Fires, Air, Road and Rail Accidents, Boat Capsizing and Village Fire have been included in this sub-group by HPC.

5. Sub-Group V–Biologically Related Disasters

This sub-group includes Biological Disasters and Epidemics, Pest Attacks, Cattle epidemics and Food poisoning. Here we will, however, discuss such natural and man-made disasters.

Table 1.2: Disasters Occurring in Different States & Union Erritories in India

S.N.	*Name of State/ UT*	*Cycl-one*	*Land-slide*	*Flood*	*Drou-ght*	*Forest fire*	*Earth-quake*	*Total*
01.	Andhra Pradesh	✓	...	✓	✓	...	....	3
02.	Arunachal Pradesh	...	....	✓	...	...	✓	2
03.	Assam	...	...	✓	....	....	✓	2
04.	Bihar including Jharkhand	...	...	✓	✓	...	✓	3
05.	Goa	...	....	....	...	...	....	...
06.	Gujarat	...	...	✓	✓	...	...	2
07.	Haryana	... .	...	✓	✓	...	...	2
08.	Himachal Pradesh	...	✓	✓	✓	✓	✓	5
09.	Jammu and Kashmir	...	✓	✓	✓	...	✓	4
10.	Karnataka	...	...	...	✓	...	...	1
11.	Kerala	...	✓	✓	✓	...	...	3
12.	Madhya Pradesh including Chhattisgarh	...	....	....	✓	...	...	1
13.	Maharashtra	....	...	✓	✓	....	✓	3
14.	Manipur	...	✓	✓	...	...	.....	2
15.	Meghalaya	...	✓	✓	....	...	✓	3
16.	Mizoram	...	...	✓	...	...	✓	2
17.	Nagaland	...	...	✓	...	...	✓	2
18.	Orissa	✓	....	✓	✓	...	✓	3
19.	Punjab	...	...	✓	✓	...	✓	3
20.	Rajasthan	...	...	...	✓	....	...	1
21.	Sikkim	...	✓	✓	...	...	✓	3
22.	Tamil Nadu	✓	....	...	✓	✓	...	3
23.	Tripura	...	...	✓	...	...	✓	2
24.	Uttar Pradesh including Uttarakhand	...	✓	...	✓	✓	✓	5

25.	West Bengal	✓	...	✓	✓	...	✓	4
26.	• Andaman and Nicobar	✓	...	✓	...	...	...	2
27.	Chandigarh	...	...	....	...	...	...	...
28.	Dadar and Nagar Haveli	....	....	.....	...	...	...	...
29.	Daman Diu	...	...	.....	....	...	....	...
30.	• Delhi							
31.	Lakshadweep	...	....	...	...	...	...	...
32.	Pondicherry	....	...	....	...	...	...	...

DISASTER MANAGEMENT SYSTEM IN INDIA

Indeed, concurrent to these occurrences, the government at various levels too, has responded by taking appropriate measures for prevention and mitigation of the effects of disasters. While long-term preventive and preparedness measures have been taken up, the unprecedented nature of the disasters has called in for a nationwide response mechanism wherein there is a pre-set assignment of roles and functions to various institutions at central, state and the district level.

The Administrative Response

At Central Level

In the federal set-up of India, the responsibility to formulate the Governments response to a natural calamity is essentially that of the concerned State Government. However, the Central Government, with its resources, physical and financial does provide the needed help and assistance to buttress relief efforts in the wake of major natural disasters. The dimensions of the response at the level of Central Government are determined in accordance with the existing policy of financing the relief expenditure and keeping in view the factors like:

(*i*) the gravity of a natural calamity,

(*ii*) the scale of the relief operation necessary, and

(*iii*) the requirements of Central assistance for augmenting the financial resources at the disposal of the State Government.

The Division of Disaster Management of Ministry of Home Affairs, Government of India is the nodal ministry for all matters concerning disasters at the Centre except the drought. The Drought Management is looked after by the Ministry of Agriculture, Government of India. The National Contingency Action Plan (NCAP) facilitates launching of relief and rescue operations without delay. The CAP identifies initiatives required to be taken by various Central Ministries, and Public Departments like in the wake of natural calamities, sets down the procedures and determines the focal points in the administrative machinery

At State Level

As pointed out earlier, the Central Government only supplements the efforts of the State Government. State Governments are autonomous in organizing relief operations in the event of natural disaster and in the long-term preparedness/ rehabilitation measures. The States have Relief Commissioners who are in charge of the relief measures in the wake of natural disasters in their respective states. In the absence of the Relief Commissioner, the Chief Secretary or an Officer nominated by him is overall in-charge of the Relief operations in the concerned State. The Chief Secretary is the head of the State Administration. The State Headquarters has, in addition, a number of Secretaries who head the various Departments handling specific subjects under the overall supervision and coordination of the Chief Secretary. At the level of the State Government natural disasters are usually the responsibility of the Revenue Department or the Relief Department. While important policy decisions are taken at the State Headquarters by the Cabinet of the State headed by the Chief Minister, day-today decisions involving policy matters are taken or exercised by the Secretary in the Department

At District Level

States are further divided into districts, each headed by a District Collector (also known as District Magistrate or Deputy Commissioner). It is the District Collector who is the focal point at the district level for directing, supervising and monitoring relief measures for disaster and for preparation of district level plans.

Disaster Management **Pages 17-31**
Edited by: Dr. Rabi Narayana Misra
ISBN: 978-93-88854-04-7
Edition: 2019
Published by: Discovery Publishing House Pvt. Ltd., New Delhi (India)

Chapter 2

Disaster Response Technologies

[1]Dr. K.V.S. Prasad

Introduction

Smart Emergency Response System (SERS) [69] prototype was built in the Smart America Challenge, 2013-2014, a United States government initiative. SERS has been created by a team of nine organizations led by Math Works. The project was featured at the White House in June 2014 and described by Todd Park (U.S. Chief Technology Officer) as an exemplary achievement.

The Smart America initiative challenges the participants to build cyber-physical systems as a glimpse of the future to save lives, create jobs, foster businesses, and improve the economy. SERS primarily saves lives. The system provides the survivors and the emergency personnel with information to locate and assist each other during a disaster. SERS allows to submit help requests to a MATLAB-based mission center connecting first responders, apps, search-and-rescue dogs, a 6-feet-tall humanoid, robots, drones, and autonomous aircraft and ground vehicles. The command and control center optimizes the available resources to serve every incoming requests and generates an action plan for the mission. The Wi-Fi network is created on the fly by the drones equipped with antennas. In addition, the autonomous rotorcrafts, planes, and ground vehicles are simulated with Simulink and visualized in a 3D environment (Google Earth) to unlock the ability to observe the operations on a mass scale. [70]

[1] Asst. Prof. of Management, GMR Institute, Rajam, A.P.

Within Other Professions

Practitioners in emergency management come from an increasing variety of backgrounds. Professionals from memory institutions (*e.g.*, museums, historical societies, etc.) are dedicated to preserving cultural heritage—objects and records. This has been an increasingly major component within this field as a result of the heightened awareness following the September 11 attacks in 2001, the hurricanes in 2005, and the collapse of the Cologne Archives.

To increase the potential successful recovery of valuable records, a well-established and thoroughly tested plan must be developed. This plan should emphasize simplicity in order to aid in response and recovery: employees should perform similar tasks in the response and recovery phase that they perform under normal conditions. It should also include mitigation strategies such as the installation of sprinklers within the institution. [71] Professional associations hold regular workshops to keep individuals up to date with tools and resources in order to minimize risk and maximize recovery.

Other Tools

In 2008, the U.S. Agency for International Development created a web-based tool for estimating populations impacted by disasters. Called Population Explorer the tool uses land scan population data, developed by Oak Ridge National Laboratory, to distribute population at a resolution 1 km2 for all countries in the world. Used by USAID's FEWS NET Project to estimate populations vulnerable and or imd by food insecurity, Population Explorer is gaining wide use in a range of emergency analysis and response actions, including estimating populations impacted by floods in Central America and the Pacific Ocean tsunami event in 2009.

In 2007, a checklist for veterinarians was published in the Journal of the American Veterinary Medical Association, it had two sets of questions for a professional to ask themselves before assisting with an emergency:

Absolute requirements for participation:

- Have I chosen to participate?
- Have I taken ICS training?

- Have I taken other required background courses?
- Have I made arrangements with my practice to deploy?
- Have I made arrangements with my family?

Incident Participation:

- Have I been invited to participate.
- Are my skill sets a match for the mission.
- Can I access just-in-time training to refresh skills or acquire needed new skills?
- Is this a self-support mission?
- Do I have supplies needed for three to five days of self-support?

While written for veterinarians, this checklist is applicable for any professional to consider before assisting with an emergency.

INTERNATIONAL ORGANIZATIONS

The International Emergency Management Society

The International Emergency Management Society (TIEMS), is an international non-profit NGO, registered in Belgium. TIEMS is a Global Forum for Education, Training, Certification and Policy in Emergency and Disaster Management. TIEMS' goal is to develop and bring modern emergency management tools, and techniques into practice, through the exchange of information, methodology innovations and new technologies.

TIEMS provides a platform for stakeholders to meet, network and learn about new technical and operational methodologies. TIEMS focuses on cultural differences to be understood and included in the society's events, education and research programs. This is achieved by establishing local chapters worldwide. Today, TIEMS has chapters in Benelux, Romania, Finland, Italy, Middle East and North Africa (MENA), Iraq, India, Korea, Japan and China.

The International Association of Emergency Managers (IAEM) is a non-profit educational organization aimed at promoting the goals of saving lives and property protection during emergencies. The mission of IAEM is to serve its members by providing information, networking and professional opportunities, and to advance the emergency management profession. It has seven councils around the world: Asia, [74] Canada, [75] Europa, [76] International, [77] Oceania, [78] Student [79] and USA. [80]

The Air Force Emergency Management Association, affiliated by membership with the IAEM, provides emergency management information and networking for U.S. Air Force Emergency Management personnel.

International Recovery Platform

The International Recovery Platform (IRP) was conceived at the World Conference on Disaster Reduction (WCDR) in Kobe, Hyogo, Japan in January 2005, as part of the Hyogo Framework for Action (HFA) 2005-2015. The HFA is a global plan for disaster risk reduction adopted by 168 governments.

The key role of IRP is to identify gaps in post disaster recovery and to serve as a catalyst for the development of tools and resources for recovery efforts. [81]

The International Red Cross and Red Crescent Movement

The International Federation of Red Cross and Red Crescent Societies (IFRC) works closely with National Red Cross and Red Crescent societies in responding to emergencies, many times playing a pivotal role. In addition, the IFRC may deploy assessment teams, *e.g.* Field Assessment and Coordination Teams (FACT),[82] to the affected country if requested by the national society. After assessing the needs, Emergency Response Units (ERUs)[83] may be deployed to the affected country or region. They are specialized in the response component of the emergency management framework.

Baptist Global Response

Baptist Global Response (BGR) is a disaster relief and community development organization. BGR and its partners respond globally to people with critical needs worldwide, whether those needs arise from chronic conditions or acute crises such as natural disasters. While BGR is not an official entity of the Southern Baptist Convention, it is rooted in Southern Baptist life and is the international partnership of Southern Baptist Disaster Relief teams, which operate primarily in the US and Canada. [84]

United Nations

The United Nations system rests with the Resident Coordinator within the affected country. However, in practice, the UN response will be coordinated by the UN Office for the Coordination of Humanitarian Affairs (UN-OCHA), by deploying a UN Disaster Assessment and Coordination (UNDAC) team, in response to a request by the affected country's government.

World Bank

Since 1980, the World Bank has approved more than 500 projects related to disaster management, dealing with both disaster mitigation as well as reconstruction projects, amounting to more than US$40 billion. These projects have taken place all over the world, in countries such as Argentina, Bangladesh, Colombia, Haiti, India, Mexico, Turkey and Vietnam. [85][85]

Prevention and mitigation projects include forest fire prevention measures, such as early warning measures and education campaigns; early-warning systems for hurricanes; flood prevention mechanisms (*e.g.* shore protection, terracing, etc.); and earthquake-prone construction. In a joint venture with Columbia University under the umbrella of the ProVention Consortium the World Bank has established a Global Risk Analysis of Natural Disaster Hotspots. [86]

In June 2006, the World Bank, in response to the HFA, established the Global Facility for Disaster Reduction and Recovery (GFDRR), a partnership with other aid donors to reduce disaster losses. GFDRR helps developing countries fund development projects and programs that enhance local capacities for disaster prevention and emergency preparedness. [87]

European Union

In 2001 the EU adopted Community Mechanism for Civil Protection, to facilitate cooperation in the event of major emergencies requiring urgent response actions. This also applies to situations where there may be an imminent threat as well. [88]

The heart of the Mechanism is the Monitoring and Information Center (MIC), part of the European Commission's Directorate-General for Humanitarian Aid & Civil Protection. Accessible 24 hours a day, it gives countries access to a one-stop-shop of civil protections available amongst all the participating states. Any country inside or outside the Union affected by a major disaster can make an appeal for assistance through the MIC. It acts as a communication hub, and provides useful and updated information on the actual status of an ongoing emergency.

NATIONAL ORGANIZATIONS

This section needs additional citations for verification. Please help improve this article by adding citations to reliable sources. Unsourced material may be challenged and removed.

Australia

Main article: Emergency Management in Australia

Naers are part of life in Australia. Heatwaves have killed more Australians than any other type of natural disaster in the 20th century. Australia's emergency management processes embrace the concept of the prepared community. The principal government agency in achieving this is Emergency Management Australia.

Canada

Public Safety Canada is Canada's national emergency management agency. Each province is required to have both legislation for dealing with emergencies, and provincial emergency management agencies, typically called "Emergency Measures Organizations" (EMO). Public Safety Canada co-ordinates and supports the efforts of federal organizations as well as other levels of government, first responders, community groups, the private sector, and other nations. The Public Safety and Emergency Preparedness Act defines the powers, duties and functions of PS are outlined. Other acts are specific to individual fields such as corrections, law enforcement, and national security.

Germany

In Germany the Federal Government controls the German Katastrophenschutz (disaster relief), the Technisches Hilfswerk (Federal Agency for Technical Relief, THW), and the Zivilschutz (civil protection) programs coordinated by the Federal Office of Civil Protection and Disaster Assistance. Local fire department units, the German Armed Forces (Bundeswehr), the German Federal Police and the 16 state police forces (Länderpolizei) are also deployed during disaster relief operations.

There are several private organizations in Germany that also deal with emergency relief. Among these are the German Red Cross, Johanniter-Unfall-Hilfe (the German equivalent of the St. John Ambulance), the Malteser-Hilfsdienst, and the Arbeiter-Samariter-Burid. As of 2006, there is a program of study at the University of Bonn leading to the degree "Master in Disaster Prevention and Risk Governance". [90] As a support function radio amateurs provide additional emergency communication networks with frequent trainings.

India

A protective wall built on the shore of the coastal town of Kalpakkam, in aftermath of the 2004 Indian Ocean earthquake.

The National Disaster Management Authority is the primary government agency responsible for planning and capacity-building for disaster relief. Its emphasis is primarily on strategic risk management and mitigation, as well as developing policies and planning. [91] The National Institute of Disaster Management is a policy think-tank and training institution for developing guidelines and training programs for mitigating disasters and managing crisis response.

The National Disaster Response Force is the government agency primarily responsible for emergency management during natural and man-made disasters, with specialized skills in search, rescue and rehabilitation. [92] The Ministry of Science and Technology also contains an agency that brings the expertise of earth scientists and meteorologists to emergency management. The Indian Armed Forces also plays an important role in the rescue/recovery operations after disasters.

Aniruddha's Academy of Disaster Management (ACDM) is a non-profit organization in Mumbai, India with 'disaster management' as its principal objective.

Malaysia

In Malaysia, The National Security Council has the responsibility to handle emergency and disaster events. Ministry of Home Affairs Malaysia, Ministry of Health Malaysia and Ministry of Housing, Urban Wellbeing and Local Government Malaysia are also having responsibility in managing emergency. Several agencies are involved in emergency managements are Royal Malaysian Police, Malaysian Fire and Rescue Department, Malaysian Civil Defence Force, Ministry of Health Malaysia and Malaysian Maritime Enforcement Agency. There were also some voluntary organisation who involved themselves in emergency/disaster management such as St. John Ambulance of Malaysia, Malaysian Red Crescent Society and so on.

Nepal

The Nepal Risk Reduction Consortium (NRRC) is based on hyogo Framework and Nepal's National Strategy for Disaster Risk Management. This arrangement unites humanitarian and development partners with Government of Nepal and had identified 5 flagship priorities for sustainable disaster risk management. [93]

New Zealand

In New Zealand, depending on the scope of the emergency/ disaster, responsibility may be handled at either the local or national level. Within each region, local governments are organized into 16 Civil Defence Emergency Management Groups (CMGs). If local arrangements are overwhelmed, pre-existing mutual-support arrangements are activated. Central Government has the authority to coordinate the response through the National Crisis Management Centre (NCMC), operated by the Ministry of Civil Defence & Emergency Management (MCDEM). These structures are defined by regulation, [94] and explained in The Guide to the National Civil Defence Emergency Management Plan, 2006, roughly equivalent to the U.S. Federal Emergency Management Agency's National Response Framework.

New Zealand uses unique terminology for emergency management. Emergency management is rarely used, many government publications retaining the use of the term civil defence. For example, the Minister of Civil Defence is responsible for the MCDEM. Civil Defence Emergency Management is a term in its own right, defined by statute. [98] And disaster rarely appears in official publications, emergency and incident being the preferred terms, [99] with the term event also being used. For example, publications refer to the Canterbury Snow Event, 2002. [100]

"4Rs" is the emergency management cycle used in New Zealand, its four phases are known as: [101]

Reduction = Mitigation

Readiness = Preparedness .

Response

Recovery

Pakistan

Disaster management in Pakistan revolves around flood disasters focusing on rescue and relief. There is a dearth of knowledge and information about hazard identification, risk assessment and management, and disaster preparedness. Disaster management, development planning and environmental management institutions operate in isolation with no integrated planning, there being no central authority for integrated disaster management. State-level measures are heavily tilted towards structural aspects.

In Russia, the Ministry of Emergency Situations (EMERCOM) is engaged in fire fighting, civil defense, and search and rescue after both natural and human-made disasters.

In Somalia, the Federal Government announced in May 2013 that the Cabinet had approved draft legislation on a new Somali Disaster Management Agency (SDMA), which had originally been proposed by the Ministry of Interior. According to the Prime Minister's Media Office, the SDMA will lead and coordinate the government's response to various natural disasters. It is part of a broader effort by the federal authorities to re-establish national institutions. The Federal Parliament is now expected to deliberate on the proposed bill for endorsement after any amendments. [102]

The Netherlands

In the Netherlands the Ministry of Security and Justice is responsible for emergency preparedness and emergency management on a national level and operates a national crisis centre (NCC). The country is divided into 25 safety regions (veiligheidsregio). In a safety region, there are four components: the regional fire department, the regional department for medical care (ambulances and psycho-sociological care etc.), the regional dispatch and a section for risk- and crisis management. The regional dispatch operates for police, fire department and the regional medical care. The dispatch has all these three services combined into one dispatch for the best multi-coordinated response to an incident or an emergency. And also facilitates in information management, emergency communication and care of citizens. These services are the main structure for a response to an emergency. It can happen that, for a specific emergency, the co-operation with an other service is needed, for instance the Ministry of Defence, water board(s) or Rijkswaterstaat. The veiligheidsregio can integrate these other services into their structure by adding them to specific conferences on operational or administrative level.

All regions operate according to the Coordinated Regional Incident Management system.

United Kingdom

Following the 2000 fuel protests and severe flooding that same year, as well as the foot-and-mouth crisis in 2001, the United Kingdom passed the Civil Contingencies Act, 2004 (CCA). The CCA defined some organisations as Category 1 and 2 Responders, setting responsibilities regarding emergency preparedness and response. It is managed by the Civil Contingencies Secretariat through Regional Resilience Forums and local authorities.

Disaster Management training is generally conducted at the local level, and consolidated through professional courses that can be taken at the Emergency Planning College. Diplomas, undergraduate and postgraduate qualifications can be gained at universities throughout the country. The Institute of Emergency Management is a charity, established in 1996, providing consulting services for the government, media and commercial sectors. There are a number of professional societies for Emergency Planners including the Emergency Planning Society [103] and the Institute of Civil Protection and Emergency Management. [104]

One of the largest emergency exercises in the UK was carried out on 20 May, 2007 near Belfast, Northern Ireland: a simulated plane crash-landing at Belfast International Airport. Staff from five hospitals and three airports participated in the drill, and almost 150 international observers assessed its effectiveness. [105]

United States

Disaster Management in the United States has utilized the functional All-Hazards approach for over 20 years, in which managers develop processes (such as communication & warning or sheltering) rather than developing single-hazard or threat focused plans (*e.g.*, a tornado plan). Processes are then mapped to specific hazards or threats, with the manager looking for gaps, overlaps, and conflicts between processes.

Given these notions, emergency managers must identify, contemplate, and assess possible man-made threats and natural threats that may affect their respective locales. [106] Because of geographical differences throughout the nation, a variety of different threats affect communities among the states. Thus, although similarities may exist, no two emergency plans will be completely identical. Additionally, each locale has different resources and capacities (*e.g.*, budgets, personnel, equipment, etc.) for dealing with emergencies. [107] Each individual community must craft its own unique emergency plan that addresses potential threats that are specific to the locality. [108]

This creates a plan more resilient to unique events because all common processes are defined, and it encourages planning done by the stakeholders who are closer to the individual processes, such as a traffic management plan written by a public works director. This type of planning can lead to conflict with non-emergency, management regulatory bodies, which require development of hazard/threat specific plans, such as development of specific H1N1 flu plans and terrorism-specific plans.

In the United States, all disasters are initially local, with local authorities, with usually a police, fire, or EMS agency, taking charge. Many local municipalities may also have a separate dedicated office of emergency management (OEM), along with personnel and equipment. If the event becomes overwhelming to local government, state emergency management (the primary government structure of the United States) becomes the controlling emergency management agency. Federal Emergency Management Agency (FEMA), part of the Department of Homeland Security (DHS), is lead federal agency for emergency management. The United States and its territories are broken down into ten regions for FEMA's emergency management purposes. FEMA supports, but does not override, state authority.

The Citizen Corps is an organization of volunteer service programs, administered locally and coordinated nationally by DHS, which seek to mitigate disasters and prepare the population for emergency response through public education, training, and outreach. Most disaster response is carried out by volunteer organizations. In the US, the Red Cross is chartered by Congress to coordinate disaster response services. It is typically the lead agency handling shelter and feeding of evacuees. Religious organizations, with their ability to provide volunteers quickly, are usually integral during the response process. The largest being the Salvation Army, [109] with a primary focus on chaplaincy and rebuilding, and Southern Baptists who focus on food preparation and distribution, [110] as well as cleaning up after floods and fires, chaplaincy, mobile shower units, chainsaw crews and more. With over 65,000 trained volunteers, Southern Baptist Disaster Relief is one of the largest disaster relief organizations in the US. [111] Similar services are also provided by Methodist Relief Services, the Lutherans, and Samaritan's Purse. Unaffiliated volunteers show up at most large disasters. To prevent abuse by criminals, and for the safety of the volunteers, procedures have been implemented within most response agencies to manage and effectively use these 'SUVs' (Spontaneous Unaffiliated Volunteers). [112]

The US Congress established the Center for Excellence in Disaster Management and Humanitarian Assistance (COE) as the principal agency to promote disaster preparedness in the Asia-Pacific region.

The National Tribal Emergency Management Council (NEMC) is a non-profit educational organization developed for Tribal organizations to share information and best practices, as well as to discuss issues regarding public health and safety, emergency management and homeland security, affecting those under Indian sovereignty. NTMC is organized into Regions, based on the FEMA 10 region system. NTMC was founded by the Northwest Tribal Emergency Management Council (NWTEMC), a consortium of 29 Tribal Nations and Villages in Washington, Idaho, Oregon and Alaska.

If a disaster or emergency is declared to be terror related or an "Incident of National Significance," the Secretary of Homeland

Security will initiate the National Response Framework (NRF). The NRF allows the integration of federal resources with local, country, state, or tribal entities, with management of those resources to be handled at the lowest possible level, utilizing the National Incident Management System (NIMS).

Conclusion

The Emergency Management Institute (EMI) serves as the national focal point for the development and delivery of emergency management training to enhance the capabilities of state, territorial, local, and tribal government officials; volunteer organizations; FEMA's disaster workforce; other Federal agencies; and the public and private sectors to minimize the impact of disasters and emergencies on the American public. EMI curricula are structured to meet the needs of this diverse audience with an emphasis on separate organizations working together in all-hazards emergencies to save lives and protect property. Particular emphasis is placed on governing doctrine such as the National Response Framework (NRF), National Incident Management System (NIMS), and the National Preparedness Guidelines. [113] EMI is fully accredited by the International Association for Continuing Education and Training (IACET) and the American Council on Education (ACE). [114]

Approximately 5,500 participants attend resident courses each year while 100,000 individuals participate in non-resident programs sponsored by EMI and conducted locally by state emergency management agencies under cooperative agreements with FEMA. Another 150,000 individuals participate in EMI-supported exercises, and approximately 1,000 individuals participate in the Chemical Stockpile Emergency Preparedness Program (CSEPP). [115]

The independent study program at EMI consists of free courses offered to United States citizens in Comprehensive Emergency Management techniques. [116] Course IS-1 is entitled "Emergency Manager: An Orientation to the Position" and provides background information on FEMA and the role of emergency managers in agency and volunteer organization coordination. The EMI Independent Study (IS) Program, a Web-based distance learning program open to the public, delivers extensive online training with approximately 200 courses. It has trained more than 2.8 million individuals. The EMI IS Web site receives 2.5 to 3 million visitors a day. [117]

Disaster Management **Pages 32-43**
Edited by: Dr. Rabi Narayana Misra
ISBN: 978-93-88854-04-7
Edition: 2019
Published by: Discovery Publishing House Pvt. Ltd., New Delhi (India)

Chapter 3

River Water Floods

A Challenge to Wild Animals and Human Society!

[1]Dr. Sandhya Rani Das
[2]Prof. R.P. Sharma

Introduction

Human beings from time immemorial remained in the nature naked with hand to mouth satisfied with leaves and fruits and sometimes eating burnt animal flesh and there was no need of shelter to take rest or sleep. What a freedom enjoyed in the nature one cannot think of; even anyone thinking about it cannot desire to go to that stage now. In struggle with the nature gradually the humans controlled the nature for their own safety and enjoyment. However even today, humans unable to control today the natural disasters which comes sudden and uninformed. The only effort available for the humans is to restore normalcy as quickly as possible.

Type of Disasters

Disasters can be classified broadly in two types, (1) natural and (2) man-made disasters.

(*a*) Natural Disasters: Cyclone, floods, draught, earth quack, land slide, are the important natural disasters.

(*b*) Man-made Disasters: Fire hazards, different types of epidemics such as cholera, plague etc. Disasters cannot be predicted before -hand to take preventive measure. Of course cyclones and floods are predicted but not its direction and intensity accurately. The human beings are helpless as before, fury of nature only praying God.

---

[1]Reader in Economics, Department of Economics, Brahmapur University.
[2]Director Institute of Economic Studies, Brahmapur -760010

Damages caused by Floods

During monsoon period with heavy rains flood of water in the rivers crosses the banks and either side of the banks of the river the water overflows and damages the agricultural fields and houses in the village. The people in the villages face the following five types of difficulties:

(1) **Loss of Human Life:** When floods occur the villages on either side of the rivers not able to come to a safer place in the water die in the water and taken away by the current of the water to a distance place. People die due to suffocation.

(2) **Loss of Property:** Houses are damaged and collapsed during the floods make the people house-less. Along with it properties in the house is also lost.

(3) **Loss of Agricultural Crops:** Floods damage the standing crops and also make the unusable for agricultural purposes as they are covered by sands. As a result of this there would be shortage of agricultural products and price of the products increases beyond imagination.

(4) **Loss of Domestic Animal.** The domestic animals like cow, goat and sheep, pigs and also poultry are lost.

(5) **Loss of Wild Animals:** Floods also destroy forests and the wild animals living in the forest.

Global Scenario of Floods

Floods are worldwide phenomenon. It is heartening to note that about 80 per cent of floods of the world are concentrated in 15 countries of the world. It is found that India is in first position in the highest position having damages due to floods. The three countries at the highest affected people are in Asia. They are India, Bangladesh and China. About 4.54 per cent of populations in India face the hazards of floods annually, followed by 3.48 and 3.28 per cent in Bangladesh and China.

Estimates of World Resources Institute, published in 2015 of 15 country's percentage of effected area of floods is presented in Fig. 3.1.

FLOOD HAVOC IN INDIA

India is highly vulnerable to floods. Out of the total geographical area of 329 million hectares (mha), more than 40 mha is flood prone. Floods are a recurrent phenomenon, which cause huge loss of lives and damages to the livelihood systems. It is a cause for concern that flood related damages show an increasing trend. The average annual flood damage in the last 10 years period from 1996 to 2005 was Rs. 4745 crores as compared to Rs.1805 crores, the corresponding average for the previous 53 years. This can be attributed to many reasons including a steep increase in population, rapid urbanization growing developmental and economic activities in flood plains coupled with global warming.

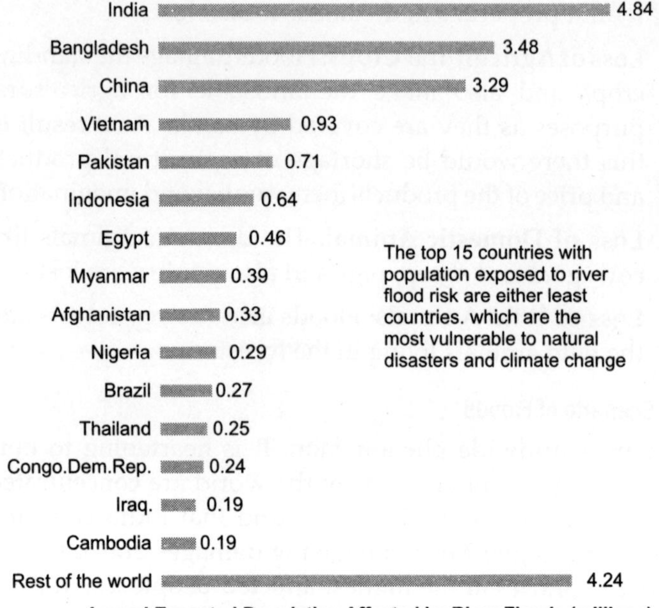

Note: An average country-wide flood protection level was assigned fer each contry based on the country's income level. 2010 population data was used in the analysis

Fig. 3.1: 15 Countries Account for 80% of Population Exposed to River Flood Risk Worldwide.

On an average every year, 75 lakh hectares of land is affected, 1600 lives are lost and the damage caused to crops, houses and public utilities is Rs.1805 crores due to floods. It is recorded that the maximum number of lives lost of 11,316 persons in the year 1977. Floods have also occurred in areas, which were earlier not considered flood prone. About eighty per cent of the precipitation takes place in the monsoon months from June to September. The rivers bring heavy sediment load from catchments. These, coupled with inadequate carrying capacity of rivers are responsible for causing floods, drainage congestion and erosion of river-banks some of the rivers causing damage in India originate in neighbouring countries; adding another complex dimension to the problem. Continuing and large-scale loss of lives and damage to public and private property due to floods indicate that we are still to develop an effective response mechanism to control floods.

The usual flood prone areas of India are shown in Map - 3.1 below. The green patches indicate the areas along with rivers are the main flood affected areas. It can be observed that all major rivers annually are flooded, with the damages of lives and land.

The flood damages in the year 2014, an average year of floods, for which detailed figures are available, are presented in Table 3.1.

Table 3.1: Annual Area Liable for Floods in India, 2015

S.No.	State	Land Million Hectors
1.	Uttar Pradesh	7.33
2.	Bihar	4.26
3.	Punjab	3.70
4.	Rajasthan	3.26
5.	Assam	3.15
6.	West Bengal	2.65
7.	Haryana	2.35
8.	Orissa	1.41
9.	Andhra Pradesh	1.39

Map 3.1 : Map of Inida Showing Flood Prone Area

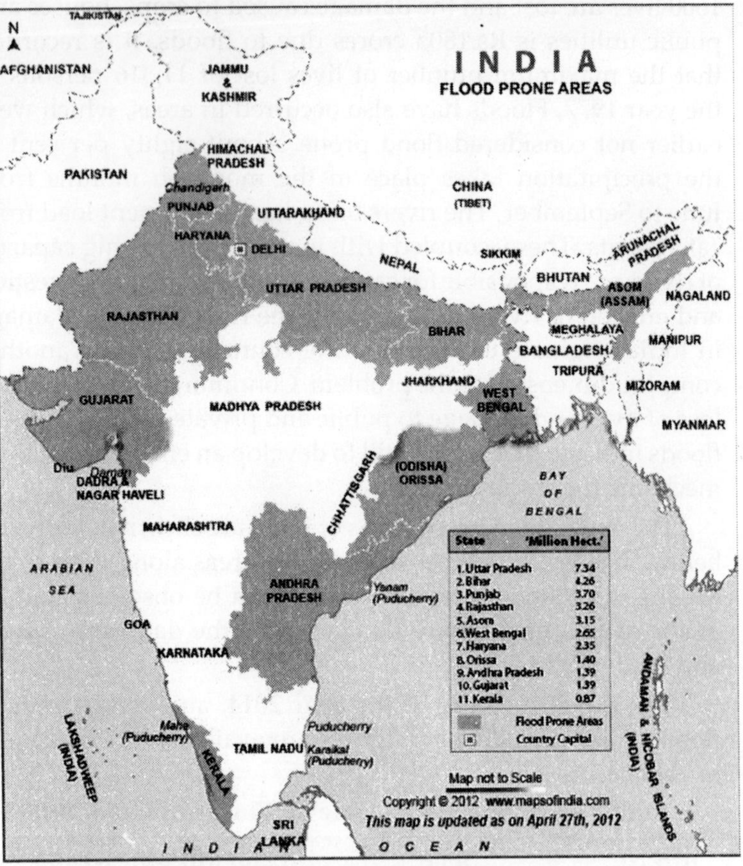

State	'Million Hect.'
1. Uttar Pradesh	7.34
2. Bihar	4.26
3. Punjab	3.70
4. Rajasthan	3.26
5. Asom	3.15
6. West Bengal	2.65
7. Haryana	2.35
8. Orissa	1.40
9. Andhra Pradesh	1.39
10. Gujarat	1.39
11. Kerala	0.87

Table 3.1: (Contd.)

10.	Gujarat	1.39
11.	Kerala	0.87
12.	Tamil Nadu	0.45
13.	Tripura	0.33
14.	Madhya Pradesh	0.26
15.	Himachal Pradesh	0.23
16.	Maharashtra	0.23
17.	Jammu & Kashmir	0.08

18.	Manipur	0.08
19.	Delhi	0.05
20.	Karnataka	0.02
21.	Meghalaya	0.02
22.	Pondicherry	0.01
	Total	**33.516**

Source : Govt. of India, Annual Flood Report, 2015.

The detail figures of damages during the floods in the states in the year 2014 are presented below:

(1) Damage of Agricultural Land: In the two of the states, Odisha and Maharashtra, the loss of agricultural land comes to 3.79 lakh hectors, that is on average about 1.90 lakh hectors.

(2) Loss in Money Terms: In four of the states, namely Assam, Meghalaya, Bengal and Kerala monetary loss the monetory loss estimated to the tune of Rs. 4042 crores that is, on an average Rs. 1010 crores per state.

(3) Persons Affected: About 51.35 lakh people were affected due to the floods, on an average about 856 lakhs per state.

(4) Loss of Lives: Deaths during the flood are available for the four of the states, namely Odisha, Meghalaya, Jammu and Kashmir, Kerala come to 355, and that is, on an average about 89 persons, but the highest death toll was in the State of Jammu and Kashmir to the number of 260 in 2014 floods.

Table 3.2: Flood Damages in India: 2014

S.N.	State	Economic Loss	People Died/ Displaced
1.	**Gujarat**	NA	20,000
2.	**Odisha**	Paddy crops on 30,659 hectare and jute and vegetable farming on 6,566 hectare damaged in 509 villages	34 persons dead, 9.95 lakh people in 1553 village of 89 blocks in 23 districts affected
3.	**Bihar**	NA	2.6 million people were affected

4.	**Assam**	Economic loss ₹ 2010 crores. Average loss of ₹ 200 crores every year	Nearly 12 lakh people
5.	**Meghalaya**	Houses, livestock etc. about ₹ 2,000 crores.	52 died
6.	**Jammu and Kashmir**	5 million people are affected	260 dead, loss of ₹ 5,400-5,700 crores.
7.	**Bengal**	Damage : ₹ 1913.66 lakh,	319,506 people affected
8.	**Kerala**	Crop loss worth ₹ 11.20 crores	29 dead, 366 people evacuated
9.	**Maharashtra**	1.4 lakh hectres farmland damaged, state lost wheat crop over 2.32 lakh hectares	NA
10.	**Karnataka**	NA	Horticultural crops lost, over 480 hectares damaged

Source: Government of India, Report on Floods in India, 2015.

Floods in Earlier Decades

According to official reports it is found that gradually less people are killed now in the floods in the country as more rescue measures are now undertaken by the government and other voluntary welfare organization in the states. Now people and media are more conscious to provide help to the flood affected area and saving more lives than earlier floods. In India between the years 1985 to 2005, there were more than 57.44 thousand deaths and more than 148.9/ lakhs of people affected due to floods. This is shown in Table 3.3.

Table 3.3: Death and Affected People in India, 1985-2005

S.No.	Year	No. Died in 000	Affected In Lakhs
1.	**1986-95**	42.03	56.15
2.	**Odisha 1999**	10.00	90.00
3.	**2005**	5.41	2.82
	Total	**57.44**	**148.97**

Source: World Disasters Report, 2006, and Odisha Report, 2000.

Floods are the regular visitors through different rivers and almost create floods in every alternative year, distrusting agriculture production and damaging houses and human, animal lives on a large scale. The average area affected by flood every year is about 8 million hectors while in some specific year total area affected in the country extended to more than 40 million hectares. The five states of Uttar Pradesh, Bihar, Assam, Bengal and Odisha are main affected states by the floods in the country which together constitute 56.10 per cent flood damages in the country. The rest 43.9 per cent is shared by other states of India. Uttar Pradesh is at the top in the flood damages and Odisha at the bottom constituting only about 4.18 per cent.

A comparative damage figure of floods in the states is shown in Fig. 3.2 below through a bar chart.

The percentage figures of damages in five Indian states are presented in Table 3.4.

Table 3.4: Sharing of Flood Damages in States, 2006

S.No.	State	Percentage of Damage
1.	Uttar Pradesh	21.90
2.	Bihar	12.71
3.	Assam	9.40
4.	Bengal	7.91
5.	Odisha	4.18
	Total	**56.10**

Source: World Disasters Report, 2006.

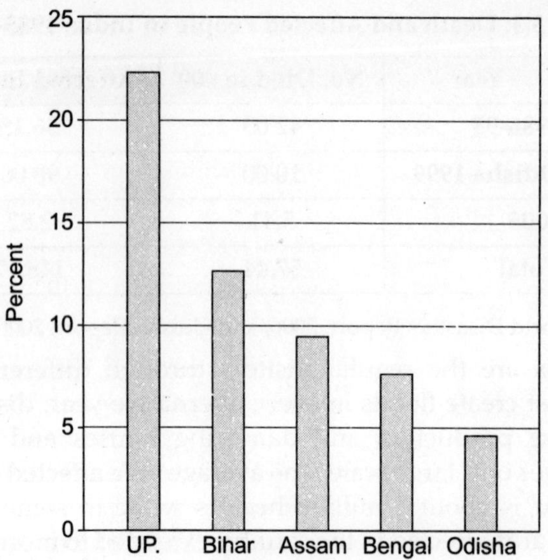

Fig. 3.2 : Flood Damages in Indian States, 2006

Flood Havoc in Recent Years

After 2014, there were floods in three states of India damaging property and killing lives on a large scale. These states are briefly reviewed:

(1) 2015 Gujarat: Heavy rain in June 2015 resulted in widespread flood in Saurashtra region of Gujarat resulting in more than 70 deaths. The wild life of Gir Forest National Park and adjoining area was also affected. Heavy rain in July resulted in widespread flood in north Gujarat resulting in more than 70 deaths.

(2) 2015 Tamil Nadu: Heavy rain in Nov.-Dec. 2015 resulted in flooding of Adyar, Cooum rivers in Chennai, resulting in financial loss and human lives.

(3) 2016 Assam: Heavy rains in July-August resulted in floods affecting 1.8 million people and flooding the Kaziranga National Park killing around 200 wild animals.

(4) 2017 Gujarat: Following heavy rain in July the state was affected by the severe flood resulting in at least 83 deaths.

Share of Floods

Floods occur in 22 of the states and Union Territories almost every year or in alternative years. Out of this 10 states are mostly flood prone. They cover 30.89 hectors annually which forms about 92 per cent of flood affected area of the country. The ten states are U.P. , Bihar, Punjab, Rajasthan, Assam, Bengal, Haryana, Odisha, Andhra Pradesh and Kerala. This is shown in a tabular form in Table-3.5.

Table 3.5: Average annual flood Affected Areas in India

S.No.	State	Land Million Hectors
1.	Uttar Pradesh	7.33
2.	Bihar	4.26
3.	Punjab	3.70
4.	Rajasthan	3.26
5.	Assam	3.15
6.	West Bengal	2.65
7.	Haryana	2.35
8.	Orissa	1.41
9.	Andhra Pradesh	1.39
10.	Gujarat	1.39
11.	Kerala	0.87
12.	Tamil Nadu	0.45
13.	Tripura	0.33
14.	Madhya Pradesh	0.26
15.	Himachal Pradesh	0.23
16.	Maharashtra	0.23

17.	Jamniu and Kashmir	0.08
18.	Manipur	0.08
19.	Delhi	0.05
20.	Karnataka	0.02
21.	Meghalaya	0.02
22.	Pondicherry	0.01
	Total	**33.52**

Source: Government of India Report, 2015.

How to Control Floods?

Full control of floods is impossible. However the dissector of floods can be partially controllable. After the heavy damage of property and life in Odisha and other parts of India due to super cyclone and floods in October 1999 were conscious and Government thought of preparing disaster management plans. For the first time a chapter on Disaster Management has been included in Tenth Five Year Plan. The Twelfth Finance Commission also mandated to review financial management for Disasters Management. The Government of India enacted The Disaster Management Act, was passed in December 2005 and accordingly The Nation Disasters Management Authority, NDMA was created by the Government of India. And accordingly Odisha is the first state to constitute Odisha State Disasters Mitigation Authority (OSDMA) in December 2000.

CONCLUSION

Higher economic development of a region if not fully control flood, but can significantly reduce human mortality and economic losses. The Government by managing pre and post flood management can reduce the damages due to floods. Construction of river embankments, maintenance of dams and reservoirs and river connectivity to channelize water from one river to the other, would help to minimize the flood impacts considerably. If sincerely those measures are under taken by the state and Central Government, to some extent the flood damages can be reduced.

SELECTED REFERENCES

Doshi, Vidhi (27 July, 2016). "Flooding in India affects 1.6m people and submerges national park". Guardian. Retrieved 2 August, 2016.

Government of India, Flood Disaster Report, 2015.

Government of India, Economic Survey, 2015-16.

Gujarat Floods: 72 people dead, over 81,000 cattle perished due to heavy rains". Firstpost. 5 August 2015. Retrieved 23 August 2015.

S.B. Easwaran (27 August 2012). "The Loudest Crash of '79". Outlook India. Retrieved 28 May, 2015.

Sonawane, Visfiakha (26 June, 2015). "Heavy Rains in India: 70 Dead in Gujarat, Flood Alert in Jammu and Kashmir". International Business Times. Retrieved 26 June, 2015.

World Bank. Environment Dept. Environmental Assessment Source Book. World Bank Publications.. Retrieved 10 January, 2012.

Disaster Management **Pages 44-58**
Edited by: **Dr. Rabi Narayana Misra**
ISBN: 978-93-88854-04-7
Edition: **2019**
Published by: **Discovery Publishing House Pvt. Ltd., New Delhi (India)**

Chapter 4

Disaster and its Management

[1]Dr. S.P. Adhikary

Introduction

The root of the word disaster derived from two Greek words *i.e.* Dis - bad and Aster - star, which symbolizes an astrological sense of calamity, blamed on the position of planets. Subsequently it was considered as the fury of nature. Now it is called a scientific phenomenon. In real sense disaster is defined as "A serious disruption of the functioning of a community or a society involving widespread human, material, economic or environmental loss and impacts, which exceeds the ability of the affected community or society to cope using its own resources".

According to Disaster Management Act, 2005 "Disaster means a catastrophe, mishap, calamity or grave occurrence affecting any area from natural and manmade causes or by accident or negligence which results in substantial loss of life or human suffering or damage to destruction of property or damage to degradation of environment and is of such a nature and magnitude as to be beyond the capacity of the community of the affected areas".

As per the WHO's definition "Any occurrence that causes damage, ecological disruption, loss of human life, deterioration of health and health services on a scale sufficient to warrant an extraordinarily response from outside the affected community or area".

[1]Dept. of Botany, Aska Scinece Collage, Aska, Odisha.

It may also defined as "A Disaster is an event that occurs in most cases suddenly and unexpectedly, causing severe disturbances to people, objects and environment, resulting in loss of life, property and health of the population. Such a situation causes disruption in normal pattern of life, generating misfortune, helplessness and suffering, affecting the socio-economic structure of a region/country to such an extent that there is a need for assistance or immediate outside intervention".

The Myths

- It Can't Happen to Us.
- The Nature's forces are so deadly the Victims will die anyway.
- There is Nothing We Can Do.

Ingredients of Disaster

- **A phenomenon or event** which constitutes a trauma for a population/environment.
- **A vulnerable point/area** that will bear the brunt of the traumatizing event.
- The **failure of local and surrounding resources** to cope with the problems created by the phenomenon.

Background

The reasons for this are varied including:

(*i*) An increasing population pressures in urban areas.

(*ii*) An increase in extend of encroachment into lands *e.g.* river beds of drainage courses, low lying areas etc.

(*iii*) Poor or ignored zoning laws and policies.

(*iv*) Large scale displacement land topography and climate.

(*v*) Lack of proper risk management (Insurance).

Factors Affecting Disaster

Factors affecting disaster divided into different types basing on host and environmental, these are as follows:

(*i*) Host factors: (*a*) age (*b*) immunization status (*c*) degree of mobility (*d*) emotional stability.

(*ii*) Environmental factors: (*a*) physical (*b*) chemical (*c*) biological (*d*) social (*e*) psychological.

Characteristic of Disaster

There are following characteristics of disaster (*i*) predictability (*ii*) controllability (*iii*) speed of onset (*iv*) length of forewarning (*v*) duration of impact (*vi*) intensity of impact.

General Effects of Disaster

(*i*) Loss of Life.
(*ii*) Injury.
(*iii*) Damage to and Destruction of Property.
(*iv*) Damage to and Destruction of Production.
(*v*) Disruption of Lifestyle.
(*vi*) Loss of Livelihood.
(*vii*) Disruption to Essential Services.
(*viii*) Damage to National Infrastructure.
(*ix*) Disruption to Governmental Systems.
(*x*) National Economic Loss.
(*xi*) Sociological and Psychological after Effect.

Types of Disaster

According to the UN International Strategy for Disaster Reduction (UN/ISDR, 2002), there are two main origins of hazards, namely (1) natural and (2) technological disasters (Man-made):

(1) **Natural disasters include three specific groups:** (*i*) **hydro-meteorological disasters:** including floods and wave surges, storms, droughts and related disasters (extreme temperatures and forest/scrub fires), and landslides and avalanches (*ii*) **geophysical disasters:** divided into earthquakes and tsunamis and volcanic eruptions (*iii*) **biological disasters:** covering epidemics and insect infestations.

(2) **The technological disasters comprise three groups, which** are: (*i*) **industrial accidents:** such as chemical spills, collapses of industrial infrastructures, explosions, fires, gas leaks, poisoning, and radiation; (*ii*) **transport accidents:** by air, rail, road or water means of transport; (*iii*) **miscellaneous accidents:** collapses of domestic/non-industrial structures, explosions, fires; (*iv*) War and civil war.

Disaster Events (1900-2009) in India

Disaster Types		Decades										
		1900 -09	1920 -29	1930 -39	1940 -49	1950-59	1960 -69	1970 -79	1980 -89	1990 -99	2000-09	Total
Hydro meteoro-logical	28	72	56	72	120	232	463	776	1498	2034	3529	8880 78.4%
Geological	40	28	33	37	52	60	88	124	232	325	354	1373 12.1%
Biological	5	7	10	3	4	2	37	64	170	361	612	1275 11.3%
Total	73	107	99	112	176	294	388	964	1900	2720	4495	11328

Natural Disaster and India

India is one of the most disaster prone countries in the world and faces following disaster and their percentage are given below: (i) Earthquake (ii) Volcanic Eruption (iii) Tsunami (iv) Cyclone (v) Flood (vi) Landslide (vii) Bushfire (viii) Drought (ix) Major Accident (Fire, Explosion, And Hazmat) (x) Civil Unrest.

Disaster Vulnerability Percentage

Over 65% land area vulnerable to earthquakes;

70% of land under cultivation prone to drought;

5% of land (40 million hectares) to floods;

8% of land mass (8,000 km coastline) to cyclones;

A Major Disaster occurs every 2-3 years;

50 million people affected annually.

1 million houses damaged annually along with human, social and other losses.

During 1985-2003, the annual average damage due to natural disasters has been estimated at 70 million US $.

Major Losses in India due to Disasters (2001-2013)

Year	Lives Lost	Cattle Lost	Houses damaged	Cropped area affected (in lakh Ha)
2001-02	834	21,269	3,46,878	18.72
2002-03	898	3,729	4,62,700	21.00
2003-04	1,992	25,393	6,82,209	31.98
2004-05	1,995	12,389	16,03,300	32.53
2005-06	2,698	1,10,997	21,20,012	35.52
2006-07	2,402	4,55,619	19,34,680	70.87
2007-08	3,764	1,19,218	35,27,041	85.13
2008-09	3,405	53,833	16,46,905	35.56
2009-10	1,677	1,28,452	13,59,726	47.13
2010-11	2,310	48,778	13,38,619	46.25

2011-12	1,600	9,126	8,76,168	18.87
2012-13	984	24,360	6,71,761	15.34
2013-14	5,677	1,02,998	12,10,227	63.74

Disaster = (Hazard + Risk) Vulnerability

Hazard

Hazard is originated from the Greek Ward "hasard" which means "luck". It is defined as a dangerous condition or natural event or man-made that could cause injury, loss of life or damage to property, livelihood or environment.

Further it could be defined as "A potentially damaging physical event, phenomenon, a human activity that may cause loss of life or injury to property damage, social and economic disruption or environmental degradation.

Characteristics

I. Location

II. Intensity

III. Frequency

IV. Probability

A hazard may turn into a disaster. All disasters are basically hazards.

Risk

Risk is defined as the probability of harmful consequence or expected or quantified losses (death, injury, properity, livelihood, economic activity) resulting from a hazard and vulnerable condition.

Total risk (Sum of the elements at risk) = Hazard × Vulnerability

In order to ascertain disaster risk we have to do HRVC analysis:

H = Hazard

R = Risk

V = Vulnerability

C = Capacity

Method:

(*i*) List out various hazards that has occurred in the community/society.

(*ii*) List out the risk associated with the listed hazards in the society/community.

(*iii*) Identify the vulnerability of the people:

(*a*) Poor

(*b*) Old, infirm

(*c*) Children

(*d*) Lactating mother

(*e*) ST/SC/Minority

(*f*) Orphan

(*g*) Houseless

(*iv*) Mapping of the capacity like:

(*a*) Trained youth

(*b*) Highland

(*c*) Strong building

(*d*) Cyclone shelters

(*e*) Hospital, availability of medicine

(*f*) Preparedness etc.

Vulnerability

Vulnerability is a set of condition resulting from physical, social, economic and environmental factors that increase the susceptibility of a community to the effects of hazard.

In other wards vulnerability is the extent to which a community can be affected by the impact of hazard due to several causes present in the community itself like poverty, lack of information, poor living condition, and inadequate safety measures.

Examples:

(*a*) Economically and socially under privileged people are more vulnerable to disaster because they live in low lying areas (flood prone). They do not have access to safe shelter, awareness education, material and opportunity to training.

(*b*) Women are more affected than men because of pregnancy and having children in arm.

(*c*) Old are more vulnerable because of health problem, inability to walk etc.

(*d*) Due to poverty migration to urban areas

Disaster = (Hazard + Risk) × Vulnerability

Resilience

It is derived from the Latin word 'resiliere' means 'to jump back'. It also defined as the ability to resile from or spring back from a 'shock'. The ability of a system, community as society exposed to hazards, to resist, absorb accommodate and to realer from the effect of a hazard in a timely and efficient manner.

Capacity/Coping Capacity

It is the specific behaviours, strategy and measures for risk reduction and management. Capacity of a community means: (*i*) Existing resources; (*ii*) Organization and training.

Capacity is existing resources *i.e.* manpower and their skill whereas resilience means putting greater emphasis on what community can do for themselves during disaster. It also emphasizes how to strengthen that capacity rather than concentrating on their vulnerability or their needs in an emergency.

Disaster Management

As per Disaster Management Act, 2005 "Disaster Management is a continuous and integrated process of planning organizing, coordinating and implementing measures which are necessary or expedient for prevention of danger or threats of disaster.

"An Applied Science which Seeks by the Systematic Observation, Analysis of Disasters, to Improve Measures Relating to Prevention, Mitigation, Preparedness, Emergency Response and Recovery."

Disaster Management Cycle

- Response
- Recovery
- Prevention & Mitigation
- Preparedness

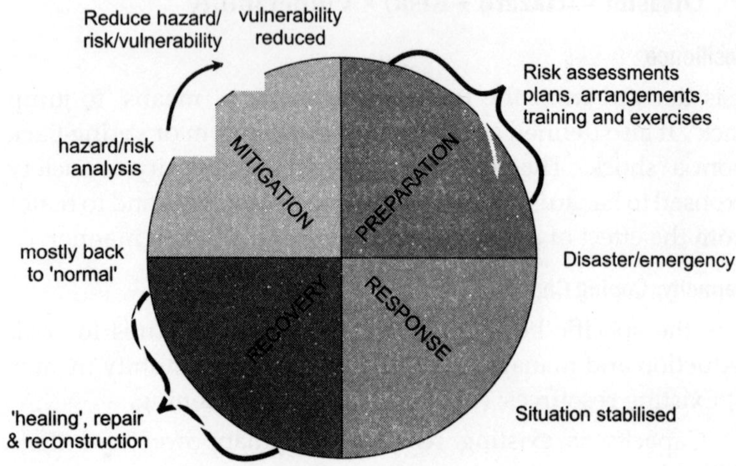

Disaster Management Cycle

Response

- Response measures are usually those which are taken immediately prior to and following disaster impact.
- Typical measures include :
  - Implementation of plans
  - Activation of the counter-disaster system
  - Search and Rescue
  - Provision of emergency food, shelter, medical assistance etc.
  - Survey and assessment
  - Evacuation measures

Recovery

- Recovery is the process by which communities and the nation are assisted in returning to their proper level of functioning following a disaster.
- Three main categories of activity are normally regarded as coming within the recovery segment:
  - (*i*) Restoration
  - (*ii*) Reconstruction
  - (*iii*) Rehabilitation

Prevention and Mitigation

- **Prevention** : Action within this segment is designed to impede the occurrence of a disaster event and/or prevent such an occurrence having harmful effects on communities or key installations.
- **Mitigation** : Action within this segment usually takes the form of specific programs intended to reduce the effects of disaster on a nation or community. For instance, some countries regard the development and application of building codes (which can reduce damage and loss in the event of earthquakes and cyclones) as being in the category of mitigation.

Preparedness

Preparedness is usually regarded as comprising measures which enable governments, organizations, communities and individuals to respond rapidly and effectively to disaster situations.

Examples of Preparedness measures are:

- The formulation & maintenance of valid, up-to-date counter-disaster plans.
- Special provisions for emergency action.
- The provisions of warning systems.
- Emergency communications.
- Public education and awareness.
- Training programs, including exercises and tests.

Principles of Disaster Management

(*a*) Risk & Hazard Assessment
(*b*) Planning
(*c*) Organization
(*d*) Resource Utilization
(*e*) Need for Specialists
(*f*) Training.

Risk and Hazard Assessment

Disaster risk will be a combination of the likelihood of the event and the vulnerability of a place to that event.

The hazard assessment will aim to deliver accurate disaster information about individual locations.

Vulnerability to a particular hazard will include:

- Critical products, services, records and operations.
- Hazardous materials.
- Potential effects of damage on stakeholders.
- Likely financial costs.
- Resources personnel and time available to make preparations.
- Level of insurance cover.

The combination of hazard and vulnerability assessments will result in formulating total risk assessment.

Planning

- to have a clear and logical approach to dealing with disasters.
- to provide common reference for all departments and authorities with roles.
- to assist with information for sitting-up a multi-functional organizational structure.
- to form a basis for coordinated action.
- to provide clear allocation of responsibilities.

- to form a basis for reviewing and evaluating current and future disaster management requirements.
- to give a focus for disaster related training.

Organization

- the nature of National Disaster Management Authority (NDMA).
- Utilization of total governmental structures/ resources *i.e.* National, State & Local level.
- Co-ordination of non-governmental resources.
- Community involvement.
- Clear lines of Authority and unity of command.
- Special system requirements.
- Emergency Operation Center/Control Center.
- Direction & Coordinating Authority.
- Communications.
- Warning Systems.
- Survey & Assessments.
- Information Management.
- Emergency Logistics.

Resource Utilization

- Identification of resources.
- Assessment of resources with relation to their capability & availability.
- Allocation of appropriate tasks.
- Level of skill in handling allotted tasks and experience.
- Activation time for deployment/availability.
- Co-ordination with line authorities of resource organizations.
- Coalition of accurate information for effective deployment of resources.

Need for Specialists

- Search & Rescue.
- Survey & Damage Assessment.
- First Aid & Triage.
- Mobile Medical & Health Team.
- Evacuation.
- Animal Husbandry/Veterinary.
- Emergency Welfare.
- Emergency Shelter.
- Emergency Logistics.
- Staff for EOC (Emergency Operating Center).
- Information Management including public information needs.
- Specialists from field of disaster studies and research Geologists, Meteorologists, etc.

Training

- Identification of Training needs.
- Scope of Training programmes.
- Training policy.
- Implementation of training.
- Design of training should be compatible to support tasks required to be performed after a Disaster at three levels: (*i*) Foundational Training; (*ii*) Team Training; (*iii*) Combined Organizational Training.

National Disaster Management Framework

- To make Disaster Management an integral part of National Development Agenda.
- To promote Awareness and Education in Disaster Management.
- To promote Human Resource Development in Disaster Management (master plan for training and capacity building).

- To develop Institutional Frameworks at the National and State levels for mainstreaming disaster management.
- To establish multi-hazard preparedness, mitigation and prevention plans at all levels.
- To enhance capacities at all levels for multi-hazard preparedness and response.

Future Direction

(*i*) Encourage and consolidate knowledge network.

(*ii*) Mobilize and train disaster volunteers for more effective preparedness, mitigation and response (NSS, NCC, Scouts, Guides, NYK, Civil defense and home guards).

(*iii*) Increased capacity building leads to faster vulnerability reduction.

(*iv*) Mobilizing stockholder participation of self help groups, women's group, youth groups and panchayati Raj Institutions.

(*v*) Anticipatory governance: Simulation exercises, Mock drill and Scenario analysis.

(*vi*) Indigenous knowledge systems and coping practices.

(*vii*) Living with risk: community based Disaster risk management.

(*viii*) Most Disasters are predictable especially in their seasonality and the disaster-prone areas which are vulnerable.

(*ix*) Communities must be involved in disaster preparedness.

(*x*) Technology driven but people owned.

(*xi*) Knowledge management: Documentation and dissemination of good practices.

(*xii*) Public private partnership.

(*xiii*) Need for special e-governance (IT Kiosks) for informed decision making in disaster-prone areas: before, during and after disasters.

(*xiv*) Disaster Nursing: It can be defined as the adaptation of professional nursing skills in recognizing and meeting the nursing, physical and emotional needs resulting from a disaster.

(*xv*) Rallies and special lectures were organized in the Universities and colleges to mark the initiatives of awareness for disaster reduction amongst youth and children.

(*xvi*) Observation of "Disaster Reduction Day" on the 12th October which is already observed by NIDM (National Institute of Disaster Management) and this activity should wide spread in the grass root level to all Govt. and Non Govt. agencies.

Disaster Management **Pages 59-68**
Edited by: **Dr. Rabi Narayana Misra**
ISBN: 978-93-88854-04-7
Edition: **2019**
Published by: **Discovery Publishing House Pvt. Ltd., New Delhi (India)**

Chapter 5

The Importance of Disaster Management

[1]P. Sunanda Vijaya Lakshmi
[2]Dr. R.N. Misra

Intruduction

There is no country that is immune from disaster, though vulnerability to disaster varies. There are four main types of disaster:

- *Natural disasters:* including floods, hurricanes, earthquakes and volcano eruptions that have immediate impacts on human health and secondary impacts causing further death and suffering from (for example) floods, landslides, fires, tsunamis.
- *Environmental emergencies:* including technological or industrial accidents, usually involving the production, use or transportation of hazardous material, and occur where these materials are produced, used or transported, and forest fires caused by humans.
- *Complex emergencies:* involving a break-down of authority, looting and attacks on strategic installations, including conflict situations and war.
- *Pandemic emergencies:* involving a sudden onset of contagious disease that affects health, disrupts services and businesses, brings economic and social costs.

Any disaster can interrupt essential services, such as health care, electricity, water, sewage/garbage removal, transportation and communications. The interruption can seriously affect the health, social and economic networks of local communities and countries. Disasters have a major and long-lasting impact

[1]Lect. in Commerce, Govt. Collage (Auto) Rajahmundry, A. P.
[2]Prof. BPCST, SMIT, Berhampur, Odisha.

on people long after the immediate effect has been mitigated. Poorly planned relief activities can have a significant negative impact not only on the disaster victims but also on donors and relief agencies. So it is important that physical therapists join established programmes rather than attempting individual efforts.

Local, regional, national and international organisations are all involved in mounting a humanitarian response to disasters. Each will have a prepared disaster management plan. These plans cover prevention, preparedness, relief and recovery.

Disaster Prevention

These are activities designed to provide permanent protection from disasters. Not all disasters, particularly natural disasters, can be prevented, but the risk of loss of life and injury can be mitigated with good evacuation plans, environmental planning and design standards. In January 2005, 168 Governments adopted a 10-year global plan for natural disaster risk reduction called the Hyogo Framework. It offers guiding principles, priorities for action, and practical means for achieving disaster resilience for vulnerable communities.

Disaster Preparedness

These activities are designed to minimise loss of life and damage - for example by removing people and property from a threatened location and by facilitating timely and effective rescue, relief and rehabilitation. Preparedness is the main way of reducing the impact of disasters. Community-based preparedness and management should be a high priority in physical therapy practice management.

Disaster Relief

This is a coordinated multi-agency response to reduce the impact of a disaster and its long-term results. Relief activities include rescue, relocation, providing food and water, preventing disease and disability, repairing vital services such as telecommunications and transport, providing temporary shelter and emergency health care.

Disaster Recovery

Once emergency needs have been met and the initial crisis is over, the people affected and the communities that support them are still vulnerable. Recovery activities include rebuilding infrastructure, health care and rehabilitation. These should blend with development activities, such as building human resources for health and developing policies and practices to avoid similar situations in future.

Disaster Management is linked with sustainable development, particularly in relation to vulnerable people such as those with disabilities, elderly people, children and other marginalised groups. Health Volunteers Overseas publications address some of the common misunderstandings about disaster management.

Affected

People who are affected, either directly or indirectly, by a hazardous event. Directly affected are those who have suffered injury, illness or other health effects; who were evacuated, displaced, relocated or have suffered direct damage to their livelihoods, economic, physical, social, cultural and environmental assets. Indirectly affected are people who have suffered consequences, other than or in addition to direct effects, over time, due to disruption or changes in economy, critical infrastructure, basic services, commerce or work, or social, health and psychological consequences. *Annotation*: People can be affected directly or indirectly. Affected people may experience short-term or long-term consequences to their lives, livelihoods or health and to their economic, physical, social, cultural and environmental assets. In addition, people who are missing or dead may be considered as directly affected.

Build Back Better

The use of the recovery, rehabilitation and reconstruction phases after a disaster to increase the resilience of nations and communities through integrating disaster risk reduction measures into the restoration of physical infrastructure and societal systems, and into the revitalization of livelihoods, economies and the environment.

Annotation: The term "societal" will not be interpreted as a political system of any country.

Building Code

A set of ordinances or regulations and associated standards intended to regulate aspects of the design, construction, materials, alteration and occupancy of structures which are necessary to ensure human safety and welfare, including resistance to collapse and damage. *Annotation:* Building codes can include both technical and functional standards. They should incorporate the lessons of international experience and should be tailored to national and local circumstances. A systematic regime of enforcement is a critical supporting requirement for the effective implementation of building codes.

Capacity

The combination of all the strengths, attributes and resources available within an organization, community or society to manage and reduce disaster risks and strengthen resilience. *Annotation:* Capacity may include infrastructure, institutions, human knowledge and skills, and collective attributes such as social relationships, leadership and management.

Coping capacity is the ability of people, organizations and systems, using available skills and resources, to manage adverse conditions, risk or disasters. The capacity to cope requires continuing awareness, resources and good management, both in normal times as well as during disasters or adverse conditions. Coping capacities contribute to the reduction of disaster risks.

Capacity assessment is the process by which the capacity of a group, organization or society is reviewed against desired goals, where existing capacities are identified for maintenance or strengthening and capacity gaps are identified for further action.

Capacity development is the process by which people, organizations and society systematically stimulate and develop their capacities over time to achieve social and economic goals. It is a concept that extends the term of capacity-building to encompass all aspects of creating and sustaining capacity growth over time. It involves learning and various types of training, but also continuous efforts to develop institutions, political awareness, financial resources, technology systems and the wider enabling environment.

Contingency Planning

A management process that analyses disaster risks and establishes arrangements in advance to enable timely, effective and appropriate responses. *Annotation:* Contingency planning results in organized and coordinated courses of action with clearly identified institutional roles and resources, information processes and operational arrangements for specific actors at times of need. Based on scenarios of possible emergency conditions or hazardous events, it allows key actors to envision, anticipate and solve problems that can arise during disasters. Contingency planning is an important part of overall preparedness. Contingency plans need to be regularly updated and exercised.

Critical Infrastructure

The physical structures, facilities, networks and other assets which provide services that are essential to the social and economic functioning of a community or society.

Disaster

A serious disruption of the functioning of a community or a society at any scale due to hazardous events interacting with conditions of exposure, vulnerability and capacity, leading to one or more of the following: human, material, economic and environmental losses and impacts.

Annotations: The effect of the disaster can be immediate and localized, but is often widespread and could last for a long period of time. The effect may test or exceed the capacity of a community or society to cope using its own resources, and therefore may require assistance from external sources, which could include neighbouring jurisdictions, or those at the national or international levels.

Emergency is sometimes used interchangeably with the term disaster, as, for example, in the context of biological and technological hazards or health emergencies, which, however, can also relate to hazardous events that do not result in the serious disruption of the functioning of a community or society.

Disaster damage occurs during and immediately after the disaster. This is usually measured in physical units (*e.g.*, square meters of housing, kilometres of roads, etc.), and describes the total or partial destruction of physical assets, the disruption of basic services and damages to sources of livelihood in the affected area.

Disaster impact is the total effect, including negative effects (*e.g.*, economic losses) and positive effects (*e.g.*, economic gains), of a hazardous event or a disaster. The term includes economic, human and environmental impacts, and may include death, injuries, disease and other negative effects on human physical, mental and social well-being:

- *Small-scale disaster:* a type of disaster only affecting local communities which require assistance beybnd the affected community.
- *Large-scale disaster:* a type of disaster affecting a society which requires national or international assistance.
- *Frequent and infrequent disasters:* depend on the probability of occurrence and the return period of a given hazard and its impacts. The impact of frequent disasters could be cumulative, or become chronic for a community or a society.
- A slow-onset disaster is defined as one that emerges gradually over time. Slow-onset disasters could be associated with, *e.g.*, drought, desertification, sea-level rise, epidemic disease.
- A sudden-onset disaster is one triggered by a hazardous event that emerges quickly or unexpectedly. Sudden-onset disasters could be associated with, *e.g.*, earthquake, volcanic eruption, flash flood, chemical explosion, critical infrastructure failure, transport accident.

Disaster Loss Database

A set of systematically collected records about disaster occurrence, damages, losses and impacts, compliant with the

Sendai Framework for Disaster Risk Reduction 2015-2030 monitoring minimum requirements.

Disaster Management

The organization, planning and application of measures preparing for, responding to and recovering from disasters. *Annotation:* Disaster management may not completely avert or eliminate the threats; it focuses on creating and implementing preparedness and other plans to decrease the impact of disasters and "build back better". Failure to create and apply a plan could lead to damage to life, assets and lost revenue.

Emergency management is also used, sometimes interchangeably, with the term disaster management, particularly in the context of biological and technological hazards and for health emergencies. While there is a large degree of overlap, an emergency can also relate to hazardous events that do not result in the serious disruption of the functioning of a community or society.

Disaster Risk

The potential loss of life, injury, or destroyed or damaged assets which could occur to a system, society or a community in a specific period of time, determined probabilistically as a function of hazard, exposure, vulnerability and capacity. *Annotation:* The definition of disaster risk reflects the concept of hazardous events and disasters as the outcome of continuously present conditions of risk. Disaster risk comprises different types of potential losses which are often difficult to quantify. Nevertheless, with knowledge of the prevailing hazards and the patterns of population and socio-economic development, disaster risks can be assessed and mapped, in broad terms at least.

It is important to consider the social and economic contexts in which disaster risks occur and that people do not necessarily share the same perceptions of risk and their underlying risk factors.

Acceptable risk, or tolerable risk, is therefore an important sub-term; the extent to which a disaster risk is deemed acceptable or tolerable depends on existing social, economic, political, cultural, technical and environmental conditions. In engineering terms, acceptable risk is also used to assess and define the structural and non-structural measures that are needed in order to reduce possible harm to people, property, services and systems to a chosen tolerated level, according to codes or "accepted practice" which are based on known probabilities of hazards and other factors.

Residual risk is the disaster risk that remains even when effective disaster risk reduction measures are in place, and for which emergency response and recovery capacities must be maintained. The presence of residual risk implies a continuing need to develop and support effective capacities for emergency services, preparedness, response and recovery, together with socio-economic policies such as safety nets and risk transfer mechanisms, as part of a holistic approach.

Disaster Risk Assessment

A qualitative or quantitative approach to determine the nature and extent of disaster risk by analysing potential hazards and evaluating existing conditions of exposure and vulnerability that together could harm people, property, services, livelihoods and the environment on which they depend. *Annotation: Disaster risk assessments include:* the identification of hazards; a review of the technical characteristics of hazards such as their location, intensity, frequency and probability; the analysis of exposure and vulnerability, including the physical, social, health, environmental and economic dimensions; and the evaluation of the effectiveness of prevailing and alternative coping capacities with respect to likely risk scenarios.

Disaster Risk Governance

The system of institutions, mechanisms, policy and legal frameworks and other arrangements to guide, coordinate and oversee disaster risk reduction and related areas of policy. *Annotation:* Good governance needs to be transparent, inclusive, collective and efficient to reduce existing disaster risks and avoid creating new ones.

Disaster Risk Information

Comprehensive information on all dimensions of disaster risk, including hazards, exposure, vulnerability and capacity, related to persons, communities, organizations and countries and their assets. *Annotation:* Disaster risk information includes all studies, information and mapping required to understand the disaster risk drivers and underlying risk factors.

Disaster Risk Management

Disaster risk management is the application of disaster risk reduction policies and strategies to prevent new disaster risk, reduce existing disaster risk and manage residual risk, contributing to the strengthening of resilience and reduction of disaster losses.

Annotation: Disaster risk management actions can be distinguished between prospective disaster risk management, corrective disaster risk management and compensatory disaster risk management, also called residual risk management.

Prospective disaster risk management activities address and seek to avoid the development of new or increased disaster risks. They focus on addressing disaster risks that may develop in future if disaster risk reduction policies are not put in place. Examples are better land-use planning or disaster-resistant water supply systems.

Corrective disaster risk management activities address and seek to remove or reduce disaster risks which are already present and which need to be managed and reduced now. Examples are the retrofitting of critical infrastructure or the relocation of exposed populations or assets.

Compensatory disaster risk management activities strengthen the social and economic resilience of individuals and societies in the face of residual risk that cannot be effectively reduced. They include preparedness, response and recovery activities, but also a mix of different financing instruments, such as national contingency funds, contingent credit, insurance and reinsurance and social safety nets.

Community-based disaster risk management promotes the involvement of potentially affected communities in disaster risk management at the local level. This includes community assessments of hazards, vulnerabilities and capacities, and their involvement in planning, implementation, monitoring and evaluation of local action for disaster risk reduction.

Local and indigenous peoples' approach to disaster risk management is the recognition and use of traditional, indigenous and local knowledge and practices to complement scientific knowledge in disaster risk assessments and for the planning and implementation of local disaster risk management.

Disaster risk management plans set out the goals and specific objectives for reducing disaster risks together with related actions to accomplish these objectives. They should be guided by the Sendai Framework for Disaster Risk Reduction 2015-2030 and considered and coordinated within relevant development plans, resource allocations and programmes activities. National-level plans need to be specific to each level of administrative responsibility and adapted to the different social and geographical circumstances that are present. The timeframe and responsibilities for implementation and the sources of funding should be specified in the plan. Linkages to sustainable development and climate change adaptation plans should be made where possible.

Disaster Management Pages 69-80
Edited by: Dr. Rabi Narayana Misra
ISBN: 978-93-88854-04-7
Edition: 2019
Published by: Discovery Publishing House Pvt. Ltd., New Delhi (India)

Chapter 6

Disaster Management Support Programme

[1]Dr. K. Srinivasa Rao

Introduction

India has been traditionally vulnerable to natural disasters on account of its geo-climatic conditions. Floods, droughts, cyclones, earthquakes and landslides have been recurrent phenomena. About 60% of the landmass is prone to earthquakes of various intensities; over 40 million hectares is prone to floods; close to 5,700 km long coastline out of the 7,516 km, is prone to cyclones; about 68% of the cultivable area is susceptible to drought. The Andaman & Nicobar Islands, the East and part of West coast are vulnerable to Tsunami. The deciduous/dry-deciduous forests in different parts of the country experience forest fires. The Himalayan region and the Western Ghats are prone to landslides.

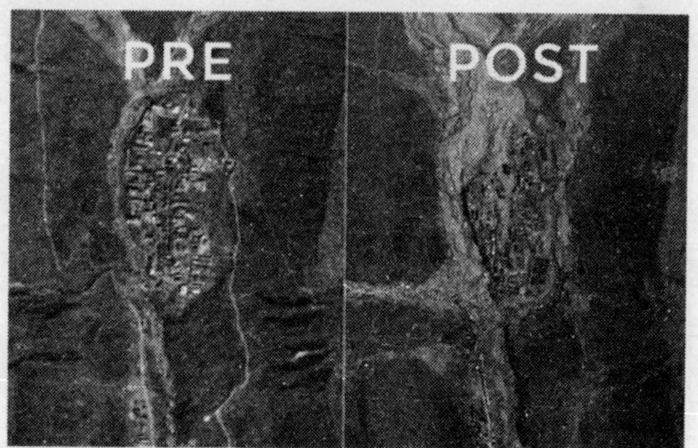

Satellite images showing the damages at Kedarnath village caused by the flash floods in June 2013

[1]Asst. Prof. Govt. Degree Collage, Ravulapalem, A.P.

Under the DMS programmes, the services emanating from aerospace infrastructure, set up by ISRO, are optimally synthesized to provide data and information required for efficient management of natural disasters in the country. The Geostationary satellites (Communication and Meteorological), Low Earth Orbiting Earth Observation satellites, aerial survey systems together with ground infrastructure form the core element of the observation Systems for disaster management. The Decision Support Centre established at National Remote Sensing Centre (NRSC) of ISRO is engaged in monitoring natural disasters such as flood, cyclone, agricultural drought, landslides, earthquakes and forest fires at operational level. The information generated from aero-space systems are disseminated to the concerned in near real time for aiding in decision-making. The value added products generated using satellite imagery helps in addressing the information needs covering all the phases of disaster management such as, preparedness, early warning, response, relief, rehabilitation, recovery and mitigation.

Flood

India is one of the most flood prone countries in the world. Floods occur in almost all rivers basins in India. Twenty-three of the 35 states and union territories in the country are subject to floods and 40 million hectares of land, roughly one-eighth of the country's geographical area, is prone to floods. Assessment of the extent of flood affected areas and the damage to the infrastructure will enable the decision-makers to plan for relief operations. Satellite based imageries due to their synoptic coverage are the best tool to assess the extent of flood affected areas. As soon as the information of a flood event is obtained, the earliest available satellite is programmesd to collect the required data for the delineation of flooded areas. Both optical and microwave satellites data is being used. The inundation maps with flooded and non-flooded areas marked in different colours along with the affected villages and the transport network are disseminated to the concerned Central / State agencies. Using the historical data of floods affecting different areas flood hazard zonation is being carried out. Such district level hazard atlases have been prepared for Assam and Bihar States. Further, integrating the information on the river morphology generated from aerial surveys, weather forecast and the *in-situ* data from CWC, flood forecasting methodologies have been generated and being operationalised.

Cyclone

The major natural disaster that affects the coastal regions of India is cyclone. India has a coastline of about 7516 kms and it is exposed to nearly 10% of the world's tropical cyclones. About 71% of this area falls in ten states (Gujarat, Maharashtra, Goa, Karnataka, Kerala, Tamil Nadu, Puducherry, Andhra Pradesh, Orissa and West Bengal). The islands of Andaman, Nicobar and Lakshadweep are also prone to cyclones. On an average, about five or six tropical cyclones form in the Bay of Bengal and Arabian sea and hit the coast every year. When a cyclone approaches to coast, a risk of serious loss or damage arises from severe winds, heavy rainfall, storm surges and river floods. Using appropriate models and satellite data, ISRO is supporting the efforts of India Meteorological Department to predict the tropical cyclone track, intensity and landfall. After the formation of cyclone, its future tracks are regularly monitored and predicted on an experimental basis using a mathematical model, developed at Space Application Centre, ISRO. These experimental track predictions are regularly posted on departmental web portal (http://www.mosdac.gov.in/scorpio/) as part of information dissemination. Using the wind pattern generated by the Oceansat-2 Scatterometer data models have been developed for predicting the formation of a cyclone even before the depression turns into a cyclone. Such cyclogenesis predictions are being carried out for all the global cyclones and uploaded to the portal.

Agricultural Drought

With more than 70 per cent of India's population relying directly or indirectly on agriculture, the impact of agricultural drought on human life and other living beings is critical. In India, around 68% of the country is prone to drought in varying degrees. Of the entire area, 35% receives rainfall between 750 mm and 1125 mm, which is considered as drought prone and 33%, receives rainfall less than 750 mm, which is considered to be chronically drought prone. Coarse resolution satellite data, which covers larger areas, is used to monitor the prevalence, severity level and persistence of agricultural drought at state/district/sub district level during kharif season (June to November). The operational methodology developed by ISRO over the years is now institutionalized by setting up Mahalanobis National Crop Forecasting Centre (MNCFC) under the Ministry of Agriculture. Currently, ISRO is concentrating on upgrading the methodology for monitoring the drought and efforts are on to develop early warning systems for agricultural drought.

Forest Fire

Nearly 55% of the total forest cover in India is prone to fires every year. An estimated annual economic loss of Rs.440 crores is reported on account of forest fires over the country. Forest fires in India have environmental significance in terms of

tropical biomass burning, which produces large amounts of trace gases, aerosol particles, and play a pivotal role in tropospheric chemistry and climate. Active forest fires are detected from the satellite images and the information is uploaded daily to the Indian Forest Fire Response and Assessment System (INFFRAS) website during the forest fire season - February to June.

Landslide

Remote sensing data have been proved to be useful for landslide inventory mapping both at local and regional level. It is also used for generating maps such as lithology, geological structure, geomorphology, land use / land cover, drainage, landslide scarp, etc. These maps can be combined with other terrain maps like slope, slope aspect, slope morphology, rock weathering and slope-bedding dip relationship in GIS environment to map the vulnerable areas for landslides. Department of Space has prepared Landslide Hazard Zonation maps (LHZ) along tourist and pilgrim routes of Uttaranchal and Himachal Pradesh, Himalayas and in Shillong-Silchar-Aizwal sector. As a part of the DSC activity all the major Landslides are being monitored for damage estimation.

Earthquakes

Remote Sensing and GIS provide a database from which the evidences left behind by disaster can be combined with other geological and topographical database to arrive at hazard map. The area affected by earthquakes are generally large, but they are restricted to well known regions (Plate contacts). Satellite data gives synoptic overview of the area affected by the disaster. These data can be made use to create a very large scale base information of the terrain for carrying out the disaster assessment and for relief measures.

Organisations involved in disaster management

Disaster Management is a complex process involving international, national and local organisations each with a distinct role to play. To respond to disaster situations a coordinated effort is required:

- The United Nations and its organisations.
- Health Care in Danger project.
- The International Federation of Red Cross and Red Crescent Societies.
- The International Committee of the Red Cross.
- International non-governmental agencies.
- National organisations.

The *Office for the Coordination of Humanitarian Affairs* (OCHA) in collaboration with the Inter-Agency Standing Committee (IASC) is the arm of the United Nations responsible for bringing together national and international humanitarian providers to ensure a coherent response to emergencies.

OCHA also ensures that a framework is in place within which each provider can contribute to the overall response effort. It also advocates for people in need, promotes preparedness and prevention and facilitates sustainable solutions.

The *Food and Agriculture Organisation of the UN* (FAO) provides early warning of impending food crises, and assesses global food supply problems.The *International Organisation for Migration* (IOM) is an intergovernmental agency which helps transfer refugees, internally displaced persons and others in need of internal or international migration services.

The Office of United Nations High Commissioner for Human Rights (OHCHR) provides assistance and advice to governments and other actors on human rights issues, sets standards and monitors rights violations.

The *United Nations Development Programme* (UNDP) assists disaster-prone countries in contingency planning and with disaster mitigation, prevention and preparedness measures.

The *United Nations High Commission for Refugees* (UNHCR) provides international protection and assistance for refugees, stateless persons and internally displaced persons, particularly in conflict-related emergencies.

The *United Nations Children's Emergency Fund* (UNICEF) works to uphold children's rights, survival, development and protection by intervening in health, education, water, sanitation, hygiene and protection.

The *World Food Programme* (WFP) is the principle supplier of relief food aid.

The *World Health Organization* (WHO) provides global public health leadership by setting standards, monitoring health trends, and providing direction on emergency health issues. WHO's role is to reduce avoidable loss of life and the burden of disease and disability. A range of *technical guidelines for health action in crises* and pre-deployment *training courses* are available. A set of technical hazard sheets on *earthquakes, drought, floods* and *landslides,* is also available.

Publications include the *Responsibilities of health-care personnel working in armed conflict and other emergencies and Ethical Principles of health care in times of armed conflict and other emergencies* which WCPT supports.

Health Care in Danger project: new e-learning module (November 2014). The module introduces health personnel to the principles underpinning ethical considerations when working in conflict situations and other emergencies. Using a multimedia interface, the module presents various dilemmas that health personnel face every day. Users can explore these issues in depth by interacting virtually with experts in the field, studying real-life issues, and receiving guidance that helps them to make decisions in difficult situations.

The International Federation of Red Cross and Red Crescent Societies

The *International Federation of Red Cross and Red Crescent Societies* is the world's largest humanitarian organization made up of 186 member Red Cross and Red Crescent Societies. The International Federation's mission is to improve the lives of vulnerable people by mobilizing the power of humanity.

The IFRC coordinates and directs international assistance to victims of natural and technological disasters, to refugees and in health emergencies. It combines its relief activities with development work to strengthen the capacities of National Societies and through them the capacity of individual people. The IFRC acts as the official representative of its member societies in the international field. It promotes cooperation between National Societies, and works to strengthen their capacity to carry out effective disaster preparedness, health and social programmes.

The International Committee of the Red Cross

The *International Committee of the Red Cross* (ICRC) is a Swiss-based humanitarian organisation and founding member of the International Red Cross and Red Crescent Movement (1863). It is mandated by the international community to be the guardian and promoter of international humanitarian law, working around the world to provide assistance to people affected by violence.

The ICRC provides physical rehabilitation to people injured by explosive weapons or other types of incident. ICRC organises, in collaboration with WHO, the *Health Emergencies in Large Populations* (HELP) course to upgrade professionalism in humanitarian assistance programmes.

The ICRC runs programmes to support the development of physical therapy education and welcomes the involvement of individuals or physical therapy institutions in supporting these developments. Opportunities are added to the *working and studying abroad* page of our website

The ICRC publication *Health care in danger: the responsibilities of health-care personnel working in armed conflicts and other emergencies* provides guidance, in simple language, on rights and responsibilities in conflict and other situations of violence for health personnel.

Leading international non-governmental agencies work through volunteers to fight poverty in developing countries. Their strong role in development works side by side with the recovery from a disaster and prevention and preparedness for any future disasters.

CARE is a humanitarian organisation fighting global poverty. Women are at the heart of CARE's community-based efforts to improve basic education, prevent the spread of HIV, increase access to clean water and sanitation, expand economic opportunity and protect natural resources. CARE also delivers emergency aid to survivors of war and natural disasters, and helps people rebuild their lives. CARE works alongside poor women because, equipped with the proper resources, women have the power to help whole families and entire communities escape poverty.

Handicap International works in partnership with local organisations and government institutions. It raises awareness of both governments and the general public on disability and landmine issues, mobilises civil society and implements action in emergency situations.

Health Volunteers Overseas (HVO) is a network of health care professionals, organisations, corporations and donors united in a common commitment to improving global health through education. The website includes a *volunteer toolkit* and an informative newsletter *Volunteer Connection*.

IMA World Health is an inter-church not-for-profit organisation based in the United States of America, which partners with USAID, the World Bank and many other organisations to build sustainable health care systems.

International Rescue Committee (IRC) offers lifesaving care and life-changing assistance to refugees forced to flee from war or disaster and provides emergency response by experienced personnel for short-term assignments.

Medecins Sans Frontieres (MSF) provides medical services in emergency situations. It recruits some physical therapists and other health professionals as well as physicians.

Oxfam is an international confederation of 14 organisations working together and with partners and allies around the world to bring about lasting change. Oxfam works directly with communities and seeks to influence the powerful to ensure that poor people can improve their lives and livelihoods and have a say in decisions that affect them.

Rehabilitation International (RI) is a global network of expert professionals who work to empower people with disabilities and provide sustainable solutions for a more inclusive and accessible society. It advocates for inclusion of people with disabilities in climate change and disaster management planning.

National Organisations

Most nations have a national disaster management plan. National disaster management plans are aligned to the most commonly experienced disasters in that country or region and the resources available. Look at the disaster management plan for your country and region. Links to the national disaster management plan for *Australia* and *India* are provided here as examples.

Government funded aid programmes coordinate national responses to disasters in another country. They may also run development projects that support countries in the recovery following a disaster.

Disaster Management **Pages 81-92**
Edited by: Dr. Rabi Narayana Misra
ISBN: 978-93-88854-04-7
Edition: 2019
Published by: Discovery Publishing House Pvt. Ltd., New Delhi (India)

Chapter 7

A Typical Study on Disaster Management
"Managing the Risk of Environmental Calamity"

[1]Mr. S. Eswara Rao
[2]Dr. R.N. Misra

Introduction

Disaster management is the discipline of dealing with and avoiding both natural and man-made disasters. It involves preparedness, response and recovery in order to lessen the impact of disasters. All aspects of emergency management deal with the processes used to protect populations or organizations from the consequences of disasters, wars and acts of terrorism. Disaster management doesn't necessarily avert or eliminate the threats themselves, although the study and prediction of the threats is an important part of the field. The basic levels of emergency management are the various kinds of search and rescue activity. Disaster management can be defined as the organization and management of resources and responsibilities for dealing with all humanitarian aspects of emergencies, in particular preparedness, response and recovery in order to lessen the impact of disasters. The word 'Disaster' derives from Middle French désastre and that from Old Italian disastro, which in turn comes from the Greek pejorative prefix δυσ-, (dus-) "bad"+ αστηρ (aster), "star". The root of the word disaster ("bad star" in Greek and Latin) comes from an astrological theme in which the ancients used to refer to the destruction or deconstruction of a star as a disaster.

Disaster management has a long history, starting with Noah's mitigation strategy of building an ark to deal with the effects of the great flood. More recently, many organizations

---

[1]Lect. in Commerce, Srikakulam, A.P.
[2]Prof. MIBA, BPUT, SMIT, Berhampur, Odisha.

have implemented structured management processes. The specific methodologies cover many of the steps mentioned in this paper, specifically the section of "Disaster Planning." A first step it risk assessment which involves estimating the likelihood of occurrence of events. Estimating event probabilities is particularly challenging because of the relatively small probabilities of event occurrences. Given the probabilities of events occurring, the disaster recovery process also calls for estimating potential losses, again a challenging task given the hypothetical nature of the endeavor. Decision analysis is a method often used to facilitate calculating expected losses once the event probabilities and looses are quantified discusses both issues related to estimating probabilities, losses and one mitigation appronch - insurance - which will be discussed below in more detail.

The various prevention and mitigation measures outlined above are aimed at building up the capabilities of the communities, voluntary organisations and Government functionaries at all levels. Particular stress is being laid on ensuring that these measures are institutionalized considering the vast population and the geographical area of the country. This is a major task being undertaken by the Government to put in place mitigation measures for vulnerability reduction. This is just a beginning. The ultimate goal is to make prevention and mitigation a part of normal day-to-day life. The above mentioned initiatives will be put in place and information disseminated over a period of five to eight years. We have a firm conviction that with these measures in place, we could say with confidence that disasters like Orissa cyclone and Bhuj earthquake will not be allowed to recur in this country; at least not at the cost, which the country has paid in these two disasters in terms of human lives, livestock, loss of property and means of livelihood.

Chennai is a metropolitan city, cosmopolitan in distribution of southern Indian, and it was severely affected by floods in November 2015. It is 100 per cent man made disaster since there isn't a system for the water to flow out. The electrical system is under ground. Chennai, one of the fast growing metres, is likely affected by the lack of drainage mainly due to uncontrolled developments of concrete spaces, encroachment of major drainage channels, shrinking of marshlands, etc., though urbanization the vital factor of response for the flood risks is coupled with the climatic variability and ecological imbalances. In this incidence at least 347 people are died (official as of 10 December) and 25,912.51 crore (US$ 3.91 billion) property has damaged. (Official estimates; unofficial estimates of over 50,000 crore (US$ 7.5 billion).

1. Types of Disasters

There is no country that is immune from disaster, though vulnerability to disaster varies. There are four main types of disaster.

Natural Disasters: These disasters include floods, hurricanes, earthquakes and volcano eruptions that can have immediate impacts on human health, as well as secondary impacts causing further death and suffering from floods causing landslides, earthquakes resulting in fires, tsunamis causing widespread flooding and typhoons sinking ferries.

Environmental Emergencies: These emergencies include technological or industrial accidents, usually involving hazardous material, and occur where these materials are produced, used or transported. Large forest fires are generally included in this definition because they tend to be caused by humans.

Complex Emergencies: These emergencies involve a break-down of authority, looting and attacks on strategic installations. Complex emergencies include conflict situations and war.

Pandemic Emergencies: These emergencies involve a sudden onset of a contagious disease that affects health but also disrupts services and businesses, bringing economic and social costs.

Man-made Disaster: Disasters caused by chemical or industrial accidents, environmental pollution, transport accidents and political unrest are classified as "human-made" or "human-induced" disasters since they are the direct result of human action.

2. Disaster Management and Finance

In light of mitigation and prevention measures, the bank must choose to manage residual risk using internal mechanisms, to use transfer mechanisms available in the insurance and capital markets, or to manage risk using some combination of these options. Managing the risk in-house could require a rigorous assessment of the effectiveness of existing disaster-related loan provisions.

3. Affects of Disaster

Hundreds of families that were living along Adyar River and other low lying areas are being evacuated as many water bodies have ruptured their banks. Transport services have been affected in the worst manner as roads are inundated and many areas in the city have been sealed off. The traffic is being diverted, thereby creating blocks. Suburban train services were also cancelled temporarily. Amidst situations like these, hope is visible in the actions of individuals helping one another in the best possible manner. And one such sight pleasantly surprised the residents of Chennai on the morning of November 11, 2015. Several roads in the city had been severely damaged due to the heavy rains. But three policemen decided to fight against the weather and help commuters reach their destination by volunteering to fill the pothole themselves. Passers-by on the stretch near Phoenix Mall in Velachery area of South Chennai saw the policemen carrying bricks and filling up the holes. They were using an iron bar to break the bricks and make the surface smooth.

4. National Disaster Qontext

Frequently hit by various natural disasters like Cyclones, Storm surges, Floods, Tornadoes, Droughts and other calamities. Monsoon flooding is an annual occurrence shaping lives and livelihoods. Almost 200 disaster events have occurred causing more than 700,000 deaths and leaving prolonged damage to livelihoods, infrastructure and the economy. Climate change is likely to cause significant impact in the form of severe floods, cyclones, droughts, sea level rise and salinity affecting agriculture, livelihoods, natural systems, water supply, health etc. The disaster vulnerable people demonstrates strong coping capacity to face the disaster challenges.

5. Disaster Prevention

1. Natural disasters particularly can be prevented not all the disasters, but the risk of loss of life and injury can be mitigated with:
   (*a*) Good evacuation plan.
   (*b*) environmental planning.
   (*c*) design standards.
2. Hyogo framework adopted by 168 governments a 10 year global plan for natural disasters risk reduction.
3. It offers guiding principles, priorities for action for disaster vulnerable communities.

6. Disaster Preparedness

1. Preparedness is the main weapon way of reducing the impact of disaster.
2. To minimize loss of life and damage by removing people and property from a threatened location to rehabilitation location.
3. Community based preparedness and management should be high priority in physical therapy practice management.

7. Disaster Relief

1. Disaster relief is a multipurpose agency to reduce the impact of disaster
2. Its long-term results and relief activities include: (*a*) Providing temporary shelter; (*b*) emergency health care; (*c*) rescue; (*d*) relocation; (*e*) providing food and water; (*f*) preventing disease and disability repairing vital services such as telecommunication and transport.

8. Disaster Recovery

1. Recovery activities include rebuilding infrastructure, healthcare and rehabilitation.

2. These should blond with development activities.
3. The development activities are building human resources for health and developing policies and practices to avoid similar situation in future.

9. Administration and Organization

Risk management must be implemented through existing administrative channels that may be characterized by appropriate levels of centralization and decentralization. High local autonomy allows localities to leverage local knowledge and expertise to allocate resources. Disaster risk management efforts coordinated at a higher level should return decision-making power and resources to the local level, particularly for mitigation activities. In instances of high centralization, local autonomies may have losses are funded and legally handled by the national entity. The process must also be sensitive to political pressures to guarantee that pre-approved risk management channels are not used for political gain. Even though decentralization will empower local governments, decisions regarding certain public assets must be enacted at the national level. Moreover, many municipalities may lack the economic resources to implement mitigation measures without national assistance. With these supports, granting increased power and responsibility to local levels can provide greater incentives for active risk management.

(a) The Indian Scenario for Disaster Management: India due to its geo-climatic and socio-economic condition is prone to various disasters. During the last thirty years' time span the country has been hit by 431 major disasters resulting into enormous loss to life and property. According to the Prevention Web statistics, 143039 people were killed and about 150 crore were affected by various disasters in the country during these three decades. The disasters caused huge loss to property and other infrastructures costing more than US $ 4800 crore. In India, the cyclone which occurred on 25th November, 1839 had a death toll of three lakh people. The Bhuj earthquake of 2001 in Gujarat and the Super Cyclone of Orissa on 29th October, 1999 are still fresh in the memory of most Indians and cloud burst and mudflow in Leh and surrounding areas in the morning of 6th August, 2010. The most recent natural disaster of a cloud burst resulting in flash floods and mudflow in Utterakhand and Kedarnath areas in the early hours of 16th June, 2013, caused severe damage in terms of human lives as well as property. There was a reported death toll of 1200 persons, about 5000 missing persons, 4200 pets (have economic value) 3,661 damaged houses in about 500 villages and 27,350 hectares of affected crop area**.

(*b*) India - Disaster Statistics: Data related to human and economic losses from disasters that have occurred between 1980 and 2010 (Table 1.2).

Natural Disasters from 1980-2010

No of events: 431
No of people killed: 143,039
Average killed per year: 4,614
No of people affected: 1,521,726,127
Average affected per year: 49,087,940
Economic Damage (US$ X 1,000): 48,063,830
Economic Damage per year (US$ X 1,000): 1,550,446

10. Organizations of Disaster Management

(*a*) Red Cross/Red Crescent: National Red Cross/Red Crescent societies often have pivotal roles in responding to emergencies. Additionally, the International Federation of Red Cross and Red Crescent Societies (IFRC or "The Federation") may deploy assessment teams, *e.g.* Field Assessment and Coordination Team—(FACT) to the affected country if requested by the national Red Cross or Red Crescent Society.

Source:

**Assumed Casualty by several News Papers 24 June 2013 Lucknow Edition

http://www.business-standard.com/article/currentaffairs/uttarakhand-death-toll-may-cross-reported-1-000- mark-shinde-113062400276–.html

http://www.business-standard.com/article/currentaffairs/rain-fury-death-toll-may-cross-l-000-3062200642–l.html

After having assessed the needs Emergency Response Units (ERUs) may be deployed to the affected country or region. They are specialized in the response component of the emergency management framework.

(*b*) World Bank: Since 1980, the World Bank has approved more than 500 operations related to disaster management, amounting to more than US$40 billion. These include post-disaster reconstruction projects, as well as projects with components aimed at preventing and mitigating disaster impacts, in countries such as Argentina, Bangladesh, Colombia, Haiti, India, Mexico, Turkey and Vietnam to name only a few. Common areas of focus for prevention and mitigation projects include forest fire prevention measures, such as early warning measures and education campaigns to discourage farmers from slash and burn agriculture that ignites forest fires; early-warning systems for hurricanes; flood prevention mechanisms, ranging from shore protection and terracing in rural areas to adaptation of production; and earthquake-prone construction. In a joint venture with Columbia University under the umbrella of the Prevention Consortium the World Bank has established a Global Risk Analysis of Natiral Disaster Hotspots. In June 2006, the World Bank established the Global Facility for Disaster Reduction and Rscovery (GFDRR), a longer term partnership with other aid donors to reduce disaster losses by mainstreaming disaster risk reduction in development, in support of the Hyogo Framework of Action. The facilities helps developing countries fund development projects and programmes that enhance local capacities for disaster prevention and emergency preparedness.

(*c*) India: The role of emergency management in India falls to National Disaster Management Authority of India, a government agency subordinate to the Ministry of Home Affairs. In recent years there has been a shift in emphasis from response and recovery to strategic risk management and reduction, and from a government-centered approach to decentralized community participation. The Ministry of Science and Technology, headed by Dr Karan Rawat, supports an internal agency that facilitates research by bringing the academic knowledge and expertise of earth scientists to emergency management. A group representing a public/ private has recently been formed by the Government of India. It is funded primarily by a large India-based computer company and aimed at improving the general response of communities to emergencies, in addition to those incidents which might be described as disasters. Some of the groups' early efforts involve the provision of emergency management training for first responders (a first in India), the creation of a single emergency telephone number, and the establishment of standards for EMS staff, equipment, and training. It operates in three states, though efforts are being made in making this a nation-wide effective group.

Conclusions

Apart from loss of human lives, natural disasters inflict severe damage to ecology and economy of a region. With installation of new technologies and by adopting space technology as INS AT and IRS series of satellites, India has developed an operational mechanism for disaster warning especially cyclone and drought, and their monitoring and mitigation. However, prediction of certain events likes earthquake, volcanic eruption and flood is still at experimental level. Disasters disrupt progress and destroy the hard-earned fruits of painstaking developmental efforts, often pushing nations, in quest for progress, back by several decades. Thus, efficient management of disasters, rather than mere response to their occurrence has, in recent times, received increased attention both within India and abroad. This is as much a result of the recognition of the increasing frequency and intensity of disasters as it is an acknowledgement that good governance, in a caring and civilized society, needs to deal effectively with the devastating impact of disasters.

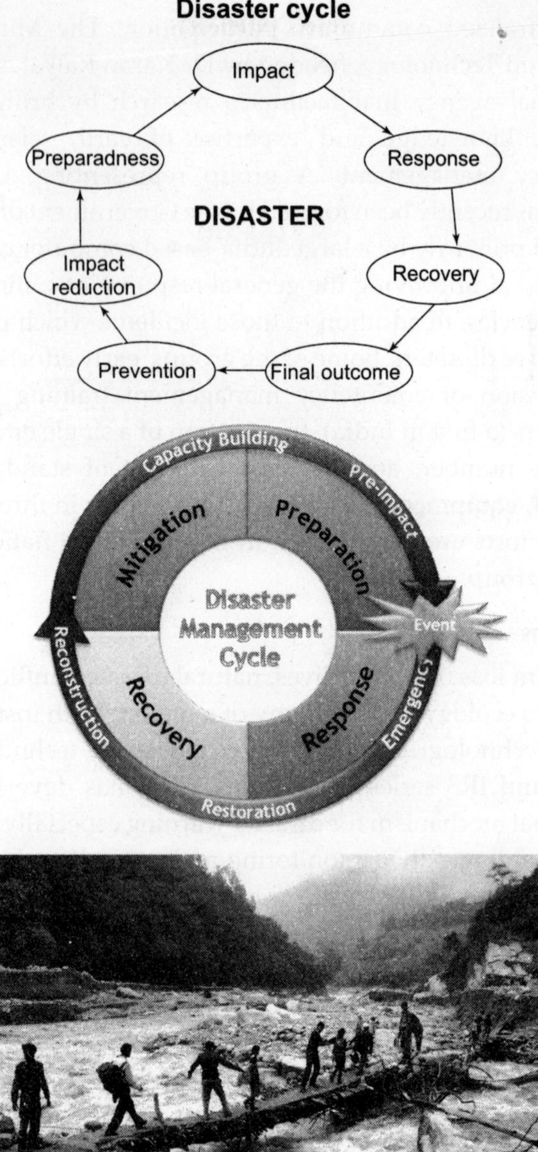

Flood Rescue

Fire Rescue

Land Slides

Tsunami

Torendo

Fire

Flood

Tsunami

Disaster Management Pages 93-104
Edited by: Dr. Rabi Narayana Misra
ISBN: 978-93-88854-04-7
Edition: 2019
Published by: Discovery Publishing House Pvt. Ltd., New Delhi (India)

Chapter 8

Disaster Risk Reduction Strategies and Policies and Early Warning System

[1]Dr. G. Chandrayya
[2]Dr. Rookesh K. Misra

Introduction

Disaster risk reduction is aimed at preventing new and reducing existing disaster risk and managing residual risk, all of which contribute to strengthening resilience and therefore to the achievement of sustainable development.*Annotation*: Disaster risk reduction is the policy objective of disaster risk management, and its goals and objectives are defined in disaster risk reduction strategies and plans.

Disaster risk reduction strategies and policies define goals and objectives across different timescales and with concrete targets, indicators and time frames. In line with the Sendai Framework for Disaster Risk Reduction, 2015-2030, these should be aimed at preventing the creation of disaster risk, the reduction of existing risk and the strengthening of economic, social, health and environmental resilience.

A global, agreed policy of disaster risk reduction is set out in the United Nations endorsed Sendai Framework for Disaster Risk Reduction, 2015-2030, adopted in March 2015, whose expected outcome over the next 15 years is: "The substantial reduction of disaster risk and losses in lives, livelihoods and health and in the economic, physical, social, cultural and environmental assets of persons, businesses, communities and countries".

---

1 Asst. Prof. Commerce, Govt. Degree Collage, Ravulapalem, A.P.
2 H.R. Manager, New Delhi.

Early Warning System

An integrated system of hazard monitoring, forecasting and prediction, disaster risk assessment, communication and preparedness activities systems and processes that enables individuals, communities, governments, businesses and others to take timely action to reduce disaster risks in advance of hazardous events.

Annotations: Effective "end-to-end" and "people-centred" early warning systems may include four interrelated key elements: (1) disaster risk knowledge based on the systematic collection of data and disaster risk assessments; (2) detection, monitoring, analysis and forecasting of the hazards and possible consequences; (3) dissemination and communication, by an official source, of authoritative, timely, accurate and actionable warnings and associated information on likelihood and impact; and (4) preparedness at all levels to respond to the warnings received. These four interrelated components need to be coordinated within and across sectors and multiple levels for the system to work, effectively and to include a feedback mechanism for continuous improvement. Failure in one component or a lack of coordination across them could lead to the failure of the whole system.

Multi-hazard early warning systems address several hazards and/or impacts of similar or different type in contexts where hazardous events may occur alone, simultaneously, cascadingly or cumulatively over time, and taking into account the potential interrelated effects. A multi-hazard early warning system with the ability to warn of one or more hazards increases the efficiency and consistency of warnings through coordinated and compatible mechanisms and capacities, involving multiple disciplines for updated and accurate hazards identification and monitoring for multiple hazards.

Economic Loss

Total economic impact that consists of direct economic loss and indirect economic loss. *Direct economic loss:* the monetary value of total or partial destruction of physical assets existing in the affected area. Direct economic loss is nearly equivalent to physical damage. *Indirect economic loss:* a decline in economic value added as a consequence of direct economic loss and/or human and environmental impacts. *Annotations:* Examples of physical assets that are the basis for calculating direct economic loss include homes, schools, hospitals, commercial and governmental buildings, transport, energy, telecommunications infrastructures and other infrastructure; business assets and industrial plants; and production such as crops, livestock and production infrastructure. They may also encompass environmental assets and cultural heritage.

Direct economic losses usually happen during the event or within the first few hours after the event and are often assessed soon after the event to estimate recovery cost and claim insurance payments. These are tangible and relatively easy to measure.

Indirect economic loss includes microeconomic impacts (*e.g.,* revenue declines owing to business interruption), mesoeconomic impacts (*e.g.,* revenue declines owing to impacts on natural assets, interruptions to supply chains or temporary unemployment) and macroeconomic impacts (*e.g.,* price increases, increases in government debt, negative impact on stock market prices and decline in GDP). Indirect losses can occur inside or outside of the hazard area and often have a time lag. As a result they may be intangible or difficult to measure.

Evacuation

Moving people and assets temporarily to safer places before, during or after the occurrence of a hazardous event in order to protect them. *Annotation:* Evacuation plans refer to the arrangements established in advance to enable the moving of people and assets temporarily to safer places before, during or after the occurrence of a hazardous event. Evacuation plans may include plans for return of evacuees and options to shelter in place.

Exposure

The situation of people, infrastructure, housing, production capacities and other tangible human assets located in hazard-prone areas. *Annotation:* Measures of exposure can include the number of people or types of assets in an area. These can be combined with the specific vulnerability and capacity of the exposed elements to any particular hazard to estimate the quantitative risks associated with that hazard in the area of interest.

Extensive Disaster Risk

The risk of low-severity, high-frequency hazardous events and disasters, mainly but not exclusively associated with highly localized hazards.

Annotation: Extensive disaster risk is usually high where communities are exposed to, and vulnerable to, recurring localized floods, landslides, storms or drought. Extensive disaster risk is often exacerbated by poverty, urbanization and environmental degradation.

Hazard

A process, phenomenon or human activity that may cause loss of life, injury or other health impacts, property damage, social and economic disruption or environmental degradation.

Annotations: Hazards may be natural, anthropogenic or socionatural in origin. **Natural hazards** are predominantly associated with natural processes and phenomena. **Anthropogenic hazards,** or human-induced hazards, are induced entirely or predominantly by human activities and choices. This term does not include the occurrence or risk of armed conflicts and other situations of social instability or tension which are subject to international humanitarian law and national legislation. Several hazards are **socionatural,** in that they are associated with a combination of natural and anthropogenic factors, including environmental degradation and climate change.

Hazards may be single, sequential or combined in their origin and effects. Each hazard is characterized by its location, intensity or magnitude, frequency and probability. Biological hazards are also defined by their infectiousness or toxicity, or other characteristics of the pathogen such as dose-response, incubation period, case fatality rate and estimation of the pathogen for transmission.

Multi-hazard means (1) the selection of multiple major hazards that the country faces, and (2) the specific contexts where hazardous events may occur simultaneously, cascadingly or cumulatively over time, and taking into account the potential interrelated effects.

Hazards include (as mentioned in the Sendai Framework for Disaster Risk Reduction, 2015-2030, and listed in alphabetical order) biological, environmental, geological, hydrometeorological and technological processes and phenomena.

Biological hazards are of organic origin or conveyed by biological vectors, including pathogenic microorganisms, toxins and bioactive substances. Examples are bacteria, viruses or parasites, as well as venomous wildlife and insects, poisonous plants and mosquitoes carrying disease-causing agents.

Environmental hazards may include chemical, natural and biological hazards. They can be created by environmental degradation or physical or chemical pollution in the air, water and soil. However, many of the processes and phenomena that fall into this category may be termed drivers of hazard and risk rather than hazards in themselves, such as soil degradation, deforestation, loss of biodiversity, salinization and sea-level rise.

Geological or geophysical hazards originate from internal earth processes. Examples are earthquakes, volcanic activity and emissions, and related geophysical processes such as mass movements, landslides, rockslides, surface collapses and debris or mud flows. Hydrometeorological factors are important contributors to some of these processes. *Tsunamis are difficult to categorize:* although they are triggered by undersea earthquakes and other geological events, they essentially become an oceanic process that is manifested as a coastal water-related hazard.

Hydrometeorological hazards are of atmospheric, hydrological or oceanographic origin. Examples are tropical cyclones (also known as typhoons and hurricanes); floods, including flash floods; drought; heatwaves and cold spells; and coastal storm surges. Hydrometeorological conditions may also be a factor in other hazards such as landslides, wildland fires, locust plagues, epidemics and in the transport and dispersal of toxic substances and volcanic eruption material.

Technological hazards originate from technological or industrial conditions, dangerous procedures, infrastructure failures or specific human activities. Examples include industrial pollution, nuclear radiation, toxic wastes, dam failures, transport accidents, factory explosions, fires and chemical spills. Technological hazards also may arise directly as a result of the impacts of a natural hazard event.

Hazardous Event

The manifestation of a hazard in a particular place during a particular period of time. *Annotation:* Severe hazardous events can lead to a disaster as a result of the combination of hazard occurrence and other risk factors.

Intensive Disaster Risk

The risk of high-severity, mid- to low-frequency disasters, mainly associated with major hazards. *Annotation:* Intensive disaster risk is mainly a characteristic of large cities or densely populated areas that are not only exposed to intense hazards such as strong earthquakes, active volcanoes, heavy floods, tsunamis or major storms but also have high levels of vulnerability to these hazards.

Mitigation

The lessening or minimizing of the adverse impacts of a hazardous event.

Annotation: The adverse impacts of hazards, in particular natural hazards, often cannot be prevented fully, but their scale or severity can be substantially lessened by various strategies and actions. Mitigation measures include engineering techniques and hazard-resistant construction as well as improved environmental and social policies and public awareness. It should be noted that, in climate change policy, "mitigation" is defined differently, and is the term used for the reduction of greenhouse gas emissions that are the source of climate change.

National Platform for Disaster Risk Reduction

A generic term for national mechanisms for coordination and policy guidance on disaster risk reduction that are multisectoral and interdisciplinary in nature, with public, private and civil society participation involving all concerned entities within a country.

Annotations: Effective government coordination forums are composed of relevant stakeholders at national and local levels and have a designated national focal point. For such mechanisms to have a strong foundation in national institutional frameworks, further key elements and responsibilities should be established through laws, regulations, standards and procedures, including: clearly assigned responsibilities and authority; building awareness and knowledge of disaster risk through the sharing and dissemination of non-sensitive disaster risk information and data; contributing to and coordinating reports on local and national disaster risk; coordinating public awareness campaigns on disaster risk; facilitating and supporting local multisectoral cooperation (*e.g.,* among local governments); and contributing to the determination of and reporting on national and local disaster risk management plans and all policies relevant for disaster risk management.

Preparedness

The knowledge and capacities developed by governments, response and recovery organizations, communities and individuals to effectively anticipate, respond to and recover from the impacts of likely, imminent or current disasters.

Annotation: Preparedness action is carried out within the context of disaster risk management and aims to build the capacities needed to efficiently manage all types of emergencies and achieve orderly transitions from response to sustained recovery.

Preparedness is based on a sound analysis of disaster risks and good linkages with early warning systems, and includes such activities as contingency planning, the stockpiling of equipment and supplies, the development of arrangements for coordination, evacuation and public information, and associated training and field exercises. These must be supported by formal institutional, legal and budgetary capacities. The related term "readiness" describes the ability to quickly and appropriately respond when required.

A preparedness plan establishes arrangements in advance to enable timely, effective and appropriate responses to specific potential hazardous events or emerging disaster situations that might threaten society or the environment.

Prevention

Activities and measures to avoid existing and new disaster risks.

Annotations: Prevention (*i.e.,* disaster prevention) expresses the concept and intention to completely avoid potential adverse impacts of hazardous events. While certain disaster risks cannot be eliminated, prevention aims at reducing vulnerability and exposure in such contexts where, as a result, the risk of disaster is removed. Examples include dams or embankments that eliminate flood risks, land-use regulations that do not permit any settlement in high-risk zones, seismic engineering designs that ensure the survival and function of a critical building in any likely earthquake and immunization against vaccine-preventable diseases. Prevention measures can also be taken during or after a hazardous event or disaster to prevent secondary hazards or their consequences, such as measures to prevent the contamination of water.

Reconstruction

The medium- and long-term rebuilding and sustainable restoration of resilient critical infrastructures, services, housing, facilities and livelihoods required for the full functioning of a community or a society affected by a disaster, aligning with the principles of sustainable development and "build back better", to avoid or reduce future disaster risk.

Recovery

The restoring or improving of livelihoods and health, as well as economic, physical, social, cultural and environmental assets, systems and activities, of a disaster-affected community or society, aligning with the principles of sustainable development and "build back better", to avoid or reduce future disaster risk.

Rehabilitation

The restoration of basic services and facilities for the functioning of a community or a society affected by a disaster.

Residual Risk

The disaster risk that remains in unmanaged form, even when effective disaster risk reduction measures are in place, and for which emergency response and recovery capacities must be maintained. *Annotation:* The presence of residual risk implies a continuing need to develop and support effective capacities for emergency services, preparedness, response and recovery, together with socio-economic policies such as safety nets and risk transfer mechanisms, as part of a holistic approach.

Resilience

The ability of a system, community or society exposed to hazards to resist, absorb, accommodate, adapt to, transform and recover from the effects of a hazard in a timely and efficient manner, including through the preservation and restoration of its essential basic structures and functions through risk management.

Response

Actions taken directly before, during or immediately after a disaster in order to save lives, reduce health impacts, ensure public safety and meet the basic subsistence needs of the people affected.

Annotation: Disaster response is predominantly focused on immediate and short-term needs and is sometimes called disaster relief. Effective, efficient and timely response relies on disaster risk-informed preparedness measures, including the development of the response capacities of individuals, communities, organizations, countries and the international community.

The institutional elements of response often include the provision of emergency services and public assistance by public and private sectors and community sectors, as well as community and volunteer participation. "Emergency services" are a critical set of specialized agencies that have specific responsibilities in serving and protecting people and property in emergency and disaster situations. They include civil protection authorities and police and fire services, among many others. The division between the response stage and the subsequent recovery stage is not clear-cut. Some response actions, such as the supply of temporary housing and water supplies, may extend well into the recovery stage.

Retrofitting

Reinforcement or upgrading of existing structures to become more resistant and resilient to the damaging effects of hazards.

Annotation: Retrofitting requires consideration of the design and function of the structure, the stresses that the structure may be subject to from particular hazards or hazard scenarios and the practicality and costs of different retrofitting options. Examples of retrofitting include adding bracing to stiffen walls, reinforcing pillars, adding steel ties between walls and roofs, installing shutters on windows and improving the protection of important facilities and equipment.

Risk Transfer

The process of formally or informally shifting the financial consequences of particular risks from one party to another, whereby a household, community, enterprise or State authority will obtain resources from the other party after a disaster occurs, in exchange for ongoing or compensatory social or financial benefits provided to that other party.

Annotation: Insurance is a well-known form of risk transfer, where coverage of a risk is obtained from an insurer in exchange for ongoing premiums paid to the insurer. Risk transfer can occur informally within family and community networks where there are reciprocal expectations of mutual aid by means of gifts or credit, as well as formally, wherein governments, insurers, multilateral banks and other large risk-bearing entities establish mechanisms to help cope with losses in major events. Such mechanisms include insurance and reinsurance contracts, catastrophe bonds, contingent credit facilities and reserve funds, where the costs are covered by premiums, investor contributions, interest rates and past savings, respectively.

Structural and Non-structural Measures

Structural measures are any physical construction to reduce or avoid possible impacts of hazards, or the application of engineering techniques or technology to achieve hazard resistance and resilience in structures or systems. Non-structural measures are measures not involving physical construction which use knowledge, practice or agreement to reduce disaster risks and impacts, in particular through policies and laws, public awareness raising, training and education.

Annotation: Common structural measures for disaster risk reduction include dams, flood levies, ocean wave barriers, earthquake-resistant construction and evacuation shelters. Common non-structural measures include building codes, land-use planning laws and their enforcement, research and assessment, information resources and public awareness programmes. Note that in civil and structural engineering, the term "structural" is used in a more restricted sense to mean just the load-bearing structure, and other parts such as wall cladding and interior fittings are termed "non-structural".

Underlying Disaster Risk Drivers

Processes or conditions, often development-related, that influence the level of disaster risk by increasing levels of exposure and vulnerability or reducing capacity.

Annotation: Underlying disaster risk drivers — also referred to as underlying disaster risk factors — include poverty and inequality, climate change and variability, unplanned and rapid urbanization and the lack of disaster risk considerations in land management and environmental and natural resource management, as well as compounding factors such as demographic change, non disaster risk-informed policies, the lack of regulations and incentives for private disaster risk reduction investment, complex supply chains, the limited availability of technology, unsustainable uses of natural resources, declining ecosystems, pandemics and epidemics.

Vulnerability

The conditions' determined by physical, social, economic and environmental factors or processes which increase the susceptibility of an individual, a community, assets or systems to the impacts of hazards.

Annotation: For positive factors which increase the ability of people to cope with hazards, see also the definitions of "Capacity" and "Coping capacity".

Disaster Management **Pages 105-119**
Edited by: Dr. Rabi Narayana Misra
ISBN: 978-93-88854-04-7
Edition: 2019
Published by: Discovery Publishing House Pvt. Ltd., New Delhi (India)

Chapter 9

Disaster Management

[1]Dr. Brajamohan Sasmal

Introduction

As per the latest information from the World Environment Controlling Authorities, the Indian Sub-Continent is among the world's most disaster prone areas. Almost 85% of the Indian states are frequently affected by natural calamities and multiple hazards like disasters. Every year, there are remarkable losses in terms of lives and properties due to the occurrence of natural types of disasters such as floods, droughts, earthquakes, tidal waves, monsoon oriented storms, landslides etc. and man-made disasters such as rapid urbanization, population explosions, ecological imbalances, changes in climates, environmental pollutions, global warming etc.

India's geo-climatic conditions as well as the high degree socio-economic and environmental degradations are highly responsible for most of the disasters. As a result of a disaster there will be extreme disruptions in functioning of the society causing human, material and environmental losses. Those losses may be compounded by every aspects of the nature of the disaster being subjected to seasonal, annual and sudden fluctuations. Of course, the unpredictability of the timings, frequency and magnitude of the occurrence of the disaster are the main factors which can cause a greater loss to the society.

A more modern and social understanding of disasters, however, views this distinction as artificial since most disasters result from the action or inaction of people and their social

[1]Prof. Chemistry (Rtd.) Berhampur-1, Odisha.

and economic structures. This happens by people living in ways that degrade their environment, developing and over populating urban centres, or creating and perpetuating social and economic systems. Communities and population settled in areas susceptible to the impact of a raging river or the violent tremors of the earth are placed in situations of high vulnerability because of their socio-economic conditions.

To control the severeness of a disaster in order to reduce the loss of human animal lives, properties and disruptions of the environment, is termed as the "Disaster Management". In recent days, the following precautionary measures are being suggested and adopted by the authorities of National Disaster Control Board, State Disaster Control Boards and District Disaster Control Boards:

1. To inform the people of a disaster occurring area by different forecasting centres, at least a weekdays time to remain well-prepared and to face the disaster boldly.
2. To remain alert and to take necessary steps for prevention of heavy losses in respect of human and animal lives, household properties and shelter places, paddy crops and the environment around the society.
3. To inform the volunteer organisations, Red Cross authorities and NGOs from time to time through the latest news agencies and RADAR communications about the severeness of the disaster in order to rescue people and pet animals from ensuing hazards of the disaster.

Classification of Disasters

The classification of disaster differs as per the criterion of classification. For example, on the basis of their origin, they arc classified as natural and man-made. If we take into account their severity, they may be classified as manor and minor disasters.

However, a high powered committee constituted in Aug. by the Government of India, under the Chairmanship of J.C. Pant adopted origin as the criterion for the classification of disaster.

The fundamental task of the committee was to prepare comprehensive model plans for disaster management at district, state and national level. The committee has identified 30 disasters and categorised them in the following five groups:

1. **Water and Climate Disaster:** Such as flood, cyclones, hailstorms, cloudburst, heat and cold waves, snow avalanches, droughts, sea erosion, thunder and lightning.
2. **Geological Disaster:** Such as landslides and mud flows, earthquakes, mine fires, dam failures and general fires.
3. **Biological Disaster:** Such as epidemics, pest attacks, cattle epidemic and food poisoning.
4. **Nuclear and Industrial Disaster:** Such as chemical and industrial disasters and nuclear accidents.
5. **Accidental Disaster:** Such as urban and forest fires, oil spill, mine flooding incidents, collapse of huge building structures, bomb blasts, air, road and rail mishaps, boat capsizing and stampede during congregations.

At central level, an administrative ministry has been identified as nodal agency for each disaster to coordinate the activities of disaster management operations at different levels.

SURVEY REPORT OF OCCURRENCE OF DIFFERENT TYPES OF DISASTERS

Earthquakes

Of the earthquake prone areas 12% is prone to very severe earthquakes, 18% to severe earthquakes and 25% to damageable earthquakes. The biggest quakes occur in the Andaman and Nicobar Islands, Kutch, Himachal and the North East. The Himalayan regions are particularly prone to earthquakes.

The last two major earthquakes shook Gujarat in January 2001 and Jammu-Kashmir in October 2005. Many smaller scale quakes occurred in other parts of India in 2006. All 7 North East states of India - Assam, Arunachal Pradesh, Nagaland, Manipur, Mizoram, Tripura and Meghalaya; Andaman & Nicobar Islands; and parts of 6 other states in the North/ North-West (Jammu and Kashmir, Uttaranchal, and Bihar) and West (Gujarat), are in Seismic Zone V.

Floods

About 30 million people are affected annually. Floods in the Indo-Gangetic Brahmaputra plains are an annual feature. On an average, a few hundred lives are lost, millions are rendered homeless and several hectares of crops are damaged every year.

Nearly 75% of the total rainfall fall occurs over a short monsoon season (June-September) 40 million hectares, or 12% of Indian land, is considered prone to floods. Floods arc a perennial phenomenon in at least 5 states – Assam, Bihar, Orissa, Uttar Pradesh and West Bengal. On account of climate change, floods have also occurred in recent years in areas that arc normally not flood prone, in 2006, drought prone parts of Rajasthan experienced floods.

Cyclones

About 8% of the land is vulnerable to cyclones of which coastal areas experience two or three tropical cyclones of varying intensity each year. Cyclonic activities on the cast coast are more severe than on the west coast.

The Indian continent is considered to be the worst cyclone-affected part of the world, as a result of low-depth ocean bed topography and coastal configuration. The principal threats from a cyclone arc in the form of gales and strong winds; torrential rain and high tidal waves/storm surges.

Most casualties arc caused due to coastal inundation by tidal waves and storm surges. Cyclones typically strike the East Coast of India, along the Bay of Bengal, *i.e.* the states of West Bengal, Orissa. Andhra Pradesh and Tamil Nadu, but also parts of Maharashtra and Gujarat at the Arabian Sea West Coast.

Landslides

Landslides occur in the hilly regions such as the Himalayas, North-East India, the Nilgiris, and Eastern and Western Ghats. Landslides in India arc another recurrent phenomenon. Landslide-prone areas largely correspond to earthquake-prone areas, *i.e.* North-west and North-East, where the incidence of landslides is the highest.

Droughts

Drought is another recurrent phenomenon which results in widespread adverse impact on vulnerable people's livelihoods and young children's nutrition status. It typically strikes arid areas of Rajasthan (chronically) and Gujarat states.

Drought is not uncommon in certain districts of Uttar Pradesh, Madhya Pradesh, Orissa. Andhra Pradesh, etc. Although a slow onset emergency, and to an extent predictable emergency, drought has caused severe suffering in the affected areas in recent years, including effects on poverty, hunger, and unemployment.

About 50 million people are affected annually by drought, of approximately 90 million hectares of rain fed areas, about 40 million hectares are prone to scanty or no rain Rainfall is poor in nine meteorological sub-divisions out of 36 sub-division (each meteorological sub-division covers a geographic area of more than ten revenue districts in India)

In India annually 33% area receive rainfall less than 750 mm (low rainfall area) and 35 % area receive between 750 to 11.25 mm rainfall Medium rainfall) and only 32 per cent falls in the high rainfall (>11. 26 mm) zone.

Cold Waves

Cold waves are recurrent phenomenon in North India. Hundreds if not thousands of people die of cold and related diseases every year, most of them from poor urban areas in northern parts of the country. According to India's Tenth Five Year Plan, natural disasters have affected nearly 6% of the population and 24% of deaths in Asia caused by disasters have occurred in India.

Between 1996 and 2001, 2% of national GDP was lost because of natural disasters, and nearly 12% of Government revenue was spent on relief, rehabilitation and reconstruction during the same period. As per a World Bank study in 2003, natural disasters pose a major impediment on the path of economic development in India.

MANAGEMENT OF DISASTERS

Under such unforeseen conditions, our managers need to plan some activities during the pre-seismic period and also discuss what should be done during the co-seismic period: Take every section of society in confidence and explain to them the limits of earthquake prediction and how the administration plans to overcome the odds.

It is a fact that the subject of earthquake prediction has not reached perfection. It is difficult to predict earthquakes. On the other hand, if the administration predicts an earthquake, and it does not occur, the administration has to face public criticism. The best way for disaster management offices is to create seismic awareness, inform people about reliable seismic precursors events and indicators that may be noted ahead of an impending earthquake.

National Disaster Management Act, 2005

National Disaster Management Act, 2005 defines events that cause substantial loss of life, prosperity and environment. It read, "Disaster means catastrophe, mishap, calamity or grave occurrence in any area, arising from nature or man-made causes, or by accident or negligence which result in substantial loss of life, of human suffering or damage to, and destruction of property, or damage to, or degradation of environment, and is of such nature or magnitude as to be beyond the coping capacity of the community of affected areas."

About 60 per cent of landmass in India is prone to earthquakes of various intensities, over — 40 million hectares is prone to floods, about 8 per cent of the total area is prone to cyclones and 68 per cent of area is susceptible to drought.

Disaster management Act, 2005 defines Disaster Management as, a continuous cycle and integrated process of planning, organizing, coordinating and implementing, measures which are necessary or expedient for (*i*) Prevention of danger or threat of any disaster; (*ii*) Mitigation or reduction of risk of any disaster or its severity or consequences; (*iii*) Capacity-building; (*iv*) Preparedness to deal with any disaster; (*v*) Prompt response to any threatening disaster situation or disaster; (*vi*) Assessing the severity or magnitude of effects of any disaster; (*vii*) Evacuation, rescue and relief; (*viii*) Rehabilitation and Reconstruction. Disaster Management Amendment Bill, 2006 aims at broadening the meaning of Disaster in Disaster Management Act.

Main Provisions of National Disaster Management Act, 2005

The Act provides for three tier mechanism for Disaster Management that includes :

National Disaster Management Authority, State Disaster Management Authority; and District Disaster Management Authority.

National Disaster Management Authority

Its chairperson is the Prime Minister. Not more than nine other members can be there. Vice Chairpersons is appointed from amongst members by the Chairperson. Executive Committee is chaired by the Secretary of the Ministry entrusted with the work of the Disaster Management.

State Disaster Management Authority

Its Chairperson is the Chief Minister of the concerned State. Other members not exceeding eight are there. And in addition, Chairperson of the State Executive Committee (who is Chief Secretary) is also included. Vice Chairperson is appointed by Chairpersons from amongst members. Chairperson of the State Executive Committee is the Chief Executive Officer. State Executive Committee is chaired by the State Chief Secretary.

National Disaster Response Fund

To be constituted by the Central Government for emergency response, relief and rehabilitation.

National Disaster Management Fund

To be constituted by the Central Government for the projects exclusively of mitigation.

Under Constitutional Position, Union List Includes

Atomic Energy, Railways etc. State List includes – Public Order, Public Health, Agriculture, Water etc. Concurrent List includes – Environment, Social Security, prevention of the extension from one State to another of infectious or contagious diseases, etc. Through State Legislative Enactments some function has been given to local government also, more so after 73rd and 74th Constitutional Amendment Act.

Union Government: Management Committee

Supportive role is there in mattes of research and development, finances, etc. There is Cabinet Committee on Management Act, 2005 provides for the National Disaster Management Authority under Prime Minister's already functional. A committee of Union government looks after issue of financial support from National Calamity Contingency Fund.

There is Central Relief Fund. Biological and Chemical Emergencies are coordinated by Cabinet Committee on security. National Crisis Management by Cabinet Committee on Security. National Crisis Management committee (NCMC) is headed by the Cabinet Secretary. Union Ministries looking after disasters arc Ministry of Home Affairs – Natural and Man-made Disasters; Ministry of Agriculture Drought, Ministry of Civil Aviation – Air Accidents; Ministry of Railways – Railway Accidents; Ministry of Environment – Chemical Disaster; Ministry of Health – Biological Disasters; Department of Atomic Energy – Nuclear Accidents; etc. Crisis Management Group (CMG) is chaired by Central Relief Commissioner in the Ministry of Home Affairs.

State Government Management Committee

Primary responsibility of relief operations is of the States. National Disaster Management Act, 2005 provides for the State Disaster Management Authority under the Chief Minister. At top political level, there is, normally Cabinet Committee on Natural Calamities under the Chief Minister.

There are Crisis Management Committees chaired by the Chief Secretaries. Relief Commissioners—functionaries of

State Revenue Department are used. They look after issues of Natural Disasters.

They work under Crisis Management Committee headed by the Chief Secretary. State Revenue Secretaries also have some responsibilities. Overall responsibility at the District Level, rests with the District Collector/ District Magistrate.

District Collector/District Magistrates

National Disaster Management Act, 2005 provides for the District Disaster Management Authority under his/her Chairpersonships (co-chairpersons is elected member of local authority). Overall co-ordinatton between various departments at district level is achieved.

Under General Financial Rules/Revenue Codes, there are powers to draw money. If there are armed forces units available locally, their assistance can be requested. Coordination with civil society is achieved.

Institution Level Management

The Disaster Management Act, 2005 has provided the legal and institutional framework for disaster management in India at the national, state and district levels. In the federal polity of India the primary responsibility of disaster management vests with the State Governments.

The Central Government lays down policies and guidelines and provides technical, financial and logistic support while the district administration carries out most of the operations in collaboration with central and state level agencies.

In the Central Government there are existing institutions and mechanisms for disaster management while new dedicated institutions have been created under the Disaster Management Act of 2005.

The Cabinet Committee on Management of Natural Calamities (CCMNC) oversees all aspects relating to the management of natural calamities including assessment of the situation and identification of measures and programmes considered necessary to reduce its impact, monitor and suggest long-term measures for prevention of such calamities, formulate and recommend programmes for public awareness for building up society's resilience to them.

The Cabinet Committee on Security. (CCS) deals with the matters relating to nuclear, biological and chemical emergencies. The National Crisis Management Committee (NCMC) under the Cabinet Secretary oversees the Command, Control and Coordination of the disaster response. The Disaster Management Act, 2005 has created new institutions at the national, state, district and local levels.

The National Disaster Management Authority (NDMA) under the Chairmanship of the Prime Minister is the apex body responsible for laying down policies, plans and guidelines for disaster management and for coordinating their enforcement and implementation throughout the country.

The policies and guidelines will assist the Central Ministries, State Governments and district administration to formulate their respective plans and programmes NDMA has the power to approve the National Plans and the Plans of the respective Ministries and Departments of Government of India. The general superintendence, direction and control of National Disaster Response Force (NDR) are vested in and will be exercised by the NDMA.

The National Executive Committee (NEC) is mandated to assist the NDMA in the discharge of its functions and further ensure compliance of the directions issued by the Central Government. The NIC comprises of the Union Norrie Secretary as the Chairperson, and the Secretaries to the CDI in the Ministries/Departments of Agriculture, Atomic Energy, Defence, Drinking Water Supply, Environment and Forests, Finance (Expenditure), Health, Power, Rural Development, Science and Technology, Space, Telecommunications, Urban Development, Water Resources and the Chief of the integrated Defence Staff of the Chiefs of Staff Committee as members.

Secretaries in the Ministry of External Affairs, Earth Sciences, Human Resource Development, Mines, Shipping, Road Transport & Highways and Secretary, NDMA arc special invitees to the meetings of the NEC.

The National Executive Committee is responsible to prepare the National Plan and coordinate and monitor the implementation of the National Policy and the guidelines issued by NDMA.

The Ministry of Home Affairs (MHA) in the Central Government has the overall responsibility for disaster management in the country. For a few specific types of disasters the concerned Ministries have the nodal responsibilities for management of the disasters, as under:

National Policy on Disaster Management, 2009

(*a*) The National Policy on Disaster Management was approved by the Government in November 2009. This comprehensive policy document lays down policies on every aspect of holistic management of disasters in the country.

Salient Features of India's National Policy on Disaster Management: India's National Policy on Disaster Management was approved by the Union Cabinet of India on 22nd October, 2009 with the aim to minimize the losses to lives, livelihoods and property, caused by natural or man-made disasters with a vision to build a safe & Disaster resilient India by developing a holistic, proactive, integrated, Multi-disaster oriented and technology driven strategy.

With this national Policy in place in India, a holistic and integrated approach will be evolved towards disaster management with emphasis on building strategic partnerships at various levels.

The themes underpinning the policy include Community based Disaster Management, Capacity development in all spheres, Consolidation of past initiatives and best practices and Cooperation with agencies at National and International levels with multi-sectoral synergy.

(*b*) The Policy is also intended to promote a culture of prevention; preparedness and resilience at all levels through knowledge, innovation and education. It encourages mitigation measures based on environmental sustainability.

It seeks to mainstream disaster management into the developmental planning process and provides for Institutional and Financial arrangements at National, State, and District-levels for Disaster Prevention, Mitigation, Preparedness and Response as it ensures adequate budgeting for disaster mitigation activities in all Ministries and Departments.

(*c*) State Policies on Disaster Management: The States of Madhya Pradesh, Gujarat, Kerala have formulated State Disaster Management Policies Tamil Nadu Chattisgarh, Uttranchal, Meghalaya, Bihar, Rajasthan, Delhi, Orissa and West Bengal have prepared draft policies.

(*d*) State Relief Codes/ DM Codes: Many States have manuals and codes for management of drought, floods etc. Now many states are in the process of changing their State Relief codes into Disaster Management Manuals.

CONCLUSION AND SUGGESTIONS

Yokhama Declaration exposed that economic loss was increasing due to various disasters. The inter-governmental Panel on that worldwide the frequency and magnitude of all types of natural disasters are increasing. Increasing tendency of droughts in some areas more vulnerability of forest fires.

Disasters affect: one, as they derail development process. Two, affects resource availability for future development. Mere narrow approach temporary relief and s more cost. There is need to link Disaster Management and Development, and Reconstruction.

Disasters—say flood-have much post-disaster complication. Man-made inhumane disasters increase. Planned Development finance for Disaster Management. Then there is targeted revenue difficult elimination issue. Over-exploitation of Natural resources is leading towards environmental degradation.

That may lead to nation increases much but public safety common sense and less in community lacks. In many instance lack of preparedness is converting hazards into disasters. Flaws in intelligence are causing some disasters, say, terrorism, strikes, social tensions, etc.

Health infrastructure is inadequate but health hazards increase. Women and children are usually most affected during disasters. More attention is needed to be given this issue. Even camp Managing Committee lack sufficient number of to take care of women, in relief and rehabilitation apprehensions of misuse of science and technological advancements exist. Drought affects rural areas more and water supply infrastructure remains weak in rural areas..

As normal procedures are difficult to follow, due to urgency corruption problems are there. In effectiveness in water mgt Policies creates problems in drought management and flood relief. Study and research in Disaster Management is still deficient. In fact, there is need to introduce the Disaster Management and Public Administration.

Traditionally, even in legal framework, meaning of disaster has been taken narrowly.

Enforcement of Public Safety Regulations is not effective low income and poverty creates problems in matters of preparedness. Professional skills for field machinery in matters of disaster management still lack:

- Still there are deficiencies in taking up the issue of Geographical Information System.
- (GIS) as a plan scheme. community participation in vulnerability analysis lacks.
- Media use for bringing mass awareness is not paid sufficient attention. Digital dissemination information by Disaster Management Authorities is still inadequate.
- Much gap exists between disaster research and community capacity building. There are instances of policy makers lacking the Disaster Management experience.
- Potentials of ex-servicemen available in between country is not used well.
- International or bilateral cooperation in Disaster management is not up to the mark.

What can be Done?

Life cycle of crisis management can be broadly divided in three phases – pre-crisis, luring crisis and post- crisis. Sustainable Development preparedness can reduce hazard. There is need to link disaster management and development plans. Planned improvement in legal framework in needed.

Bringing community consciousness will help. Short-term and long-terms planning iced integration. More effective international cooperation and use of it is need for Disaster warming system.

As normally, community response is the first in case of disaster, there is need for community capacity building. Policy of Emergency Operation Centres (EOC) at national, state and district level should be effectively implemented.

Subject of Disaster Management is not mentioned specifically, in any of the three lists of the Seventh Schedule of the constitution. National Commission of the Constitution (NCRWC) suggested its inclusion in Concurrent List. Best Practices Guidelines should be laid down.

Meaning of Disaster in National Disaster Management Act, 2005 is narrow it should be broadened. Capacity building in local government is needed. In Japan local governments have a role to play in such matters.

2nd ARC recommends, in larger cities (say with population, exceeding 2.5 million) the Mayor, assisted by the Commissioner of the Municipal Corporation and the Police Commissioner should be directly responsible for Crisis management.

Initiatives - Calamity Relief Fund (CRF) exists, Various related rules exist, say, Hazardous Waste (Management and Handling Rules), 1989, The Ozone Depleting Substances (Regulation and Control Rules, 2000 etc.

National Institute of Disaster Management is set up at Delhi., Coastal Zone Regulations, Building Codes, Fire Safety Rules etc. some States have gone for State Disaster Management Acts, say : Act, 2003, Bihar Disaster Management Act, 2004, Uttrakhand Disaster Mitigation, Management and Prevention

Act, 2005; Uttar Pradesh Disaster Management Act, 2005 etc. Uttarakhand has set up a separate department of Disaster Management.

Vulnerability Atlas of India was brought in 1998. Seismic Zone of India has been standardized. Of late, Five Year Planning had been giving high priority to such issues. National Building Code 3 was brought in 2005.

India Disaster Resources network Disaster Management A web enabled centralized data base. Standard Operating Procedures (SOP) are there which guide the operations in ease of crisis. Civil Defence Act was brought in 1968 and Civil Defence Regulations, 1968 exist.

SAARC Disaster Management Centre it was set up in October 2006. It is in the premises of National Institute of Disaster Management, New Delhi.

Disaster Management **Pages 120-132**
Edited by: Dr. Rabi Narayana Misra
ISBN: 978-93-88854-04-7
Edition: 2019
Published by: Discovery Publishing House Pvt. Ltd., New Delhi (India)

Chapter 10

Disaster Management Cycle Process

[1]Dr. G. Chandrayya
[2]Dr. D. Tata Rao

Introduction

Disaster management aims to reduce, or avoid, the potential losses from hazards, assure prompt and appropriate assistance to victims of disaster, and achieve rapid and effective recovery. The Disaster management cycle illustrates the ongoing process by which governments, businesses, and civil society plan for and reduce the impact of disasters, react during and immediately following a disaster, and take steps to recover after a disaster has occurred. Appropriate actions at all points in the cycle lead to greater preparedness, better warnings, reduced vulnerability or the prevention of disasters during the next iteration of the cycle. The complete disaster management cycle includes the shaping of public policies and plans that either modify the causes of disasters or mitigate their effects on people, property, and infrastructure.

The mitigation and preparedness phases occur as disaster management improvements are made in anticipation of a disaster event. Developmental considerations play a key role in contributing to the mitigation and preparation of a community to effectively confront a disaster. As a disaster occurs, disaster management actors, in particular humanitarian organizations, become involved in the immediate response and long-term recovery phases. The four disaster management phases illustrated here do not always, or even generally, occur in isolation or in this precise order. Often phases of the cycle

[1]Asst. Prof. Govt. Degree Collage, Rovulapalem, A.P.
[2]Principal, Govt. Degree College, *Viz.*, A.P.

overlap and the length of each phase greatly depends on the severity of the disaster.

- *Mitigation* - Minimizing the effects of disaster.
  Examples: building codes and zoning; vulnerability analyses; public education.
- *Preparedness* - Planning how to respond.
  Examples: preparedness plans; emergency exercises/ training; warning systems.
- *Response* - Efforts to minimize the hazards created by a disaster.
  Examples: search and rescue; emergency relief.
- *Recovery* - Returning the community to normal.
  Examples: temporary housing; grants; medical care.

Sustainable Development

Developmental considerations contribute to all aspects of the disaster management cycle. One of the main goals of disaster management, and one of its strongest links with development, is the promotion of sustainable livelihoods and their protection and recovery during disasters and emergencies. Where this goal is achieved, people have a greater capacity to deal with disasters and their recovery is more rapid and long lasting. In a development oriented disaster management approach, the objectives are to reduce hazards, prevent disasters, and prepare for emergencies. Therefore, developmental considerations are strongly represented in the mitigation and preparedness phases of the disaster management cycle. Inappropriate development processes can lead to increased vulnerability to disasters and loss of preparedness for emergency situations.

Mitigation

Mitigation activities actually eliminate or reduce the probability of disaster occurrence, or reduce the effects of unavoidable disasters. Mitigation measures include building codes; vulnerability analyses updates; zoning and land use management; building use regulations and safety codes; preventive health care; and public education.

Mitigation will depend on the incorporation of appropriate measures in national and regional development planning. Its effectiveness will also depend on the availability of information on hazards, emergency risks, and the countermeasures to be taken. The mitigation phase, and indeed the whole disaster management cycle, includes the shaping of public policies and plans that either modify the causes of disasters or mitigate their effects on people, property, and infrastructure.

Preparedness

The goal of emergency preparedness programmes is to achieve a satisfactory level of readiness to respond to any emergency situation through programmes that strengthen the technical and managerial capacity of governments, organizations, and communities. These measures can be described as logistical readiness to deal with disasters and can be enhanced by having response mechanisms and procedures, rehearsals, developing long-term and short-term strategies, public education and building early warning systems. Preparedness can also take the form of ensuring that strategic reserves of food, equipment, water, medicines and other essentials are maintained in cases of national or local catastrophes.

During the preparedness phase, governments, organizations, and individuals develop plans to save lives, minimize disaster damage, and enhance disaster response operations. Preparedness measures include preparedness plans; emergency exercises/training; warning systems; emergency communications systems; evacuations plans and training; resource inventories; emergency personnel/contact lists; mutual aid agreements; and public information/education. As with mitigations efforts, preparedness actions depend on the incorporation of appropriate measures in national and regional development plans. In addition, their effectiveness depends on the availability of information on hazards, emergency risks and the countermeasures to be taken, and on the degree to which government agencies, non-governmental organizations and the general public are able to make use of this information.

Humanitarian Action

During a disaster, humanitarian agencies are often called upon to deal with immediate response and recovery. To be able to respond effectively, these agencies must have experienced leaders, trained personnel, adequate transport and logistic support, appropriate communications, and guidelines for working in emergencies. If the necessary preparations have not been made, the humanitarian agencies will not be able to meet the immediate needs of the people.

Response

The aim of emergency response is to provide immediate assistance to maintain life, improve health and support the morale of the affected population. Such assistance may range from providing specific but limited aid, such as assisting refugees with transport, temporary shelter, and food, to establishing semi-permanent settlement in camps and other locations. It also may involve initial repairs to damaged infrastructure. The focus in the response phase is on meeting the basic needs of the people until more permanent and sustainable solutions can be found. Humanitarian organizations are often strongly present in this phase of the disaster management cycle.

Recovery

As the emergency is brought under control, the affected population is capable of undertaking a growing number of activities aimed at restoring their lives and the infrastructure that supports them. There is no distinct point at which immediate relief changes into recovery and then into long-term sustainable development. There will be many opportunities during the recovery period to enhance prevention and increase preparedness, thus reducing vulnerability. Ideally, there should be a smooth transition from recovery to on-going development.

Recovery activities continue until all systems return to normal or better. Recovery measures, both short and long term, include returning vital life-support systems to minimum operating standards; temporary housing; public information; health and safety education; reconstruction; counseling programmes; and economic impact studies. Information resources and services include data collection related to rebuilding, and documentation of lessons learned.

References

- Environmental health in emergencies and disasters: A practical guide. WHO, 2002.
- Disaster Help, US Department of Homeland Security.
- Green Paper on Disaster Management, Department of Provincial and Local Government, South Africa

Disaster Management Cycle

Mitigation: Measures that prevent or reduce the impact of disasters.

Preparedness: Planning, training, & educational activities for things that cant be mitigated.

Response: The immediate aftermath of a disaster, when business is not as usual.

Recovery: The long-term aftermath of a disaster, when restoration efforts are in addition to regular services.

Management (or disaster management) is the discipline dealing of with and avoiding risks. It is a discipline that involves preparing, supporting, and rebuilding society when natural or human-made disasters occur.

In general, any Emergency management is the continuous process by which all individuals, groups, and communities manage hazards in an effort to avoid or ameliorate the impact of disasters resulting from the hazards.

Actions taken depend in part on perceptions of risk of those exposed. Effective emergency management relies on thorough integration of emergency plans at all levels of government and non-government involvement. Activities at each level (individual, group, community) affect the other levels. It is common to place the responsibility for governmental emergency management with the institutions for civil defence or within the conventional structure of the emergency services, in the private sector, emergency management is sometimes referred to as business continuity management.

Mitigation

Mitigation efforts attempt to prevent hazards from developing into disasters altogether, or to reduce the effects of disasters when they occur. The mitigation phase differs from the other phases because it focuses on long-term measures for reducing or eliminating risk Personal mitigation is mainly about knowing and avoiding unnecessary risks. This includes an assessment of possible risks to personal/family health and to personal property.

An example of personal non-structural mitigation would be to avoid buying property that is exposed to hazards, *e.g.* in a flood plain, in areas of subsidence or landslides. Homeowners may not be aware of their home being exposed to a hazard until it strikes. Real estate agents may not come forward with such information. However, specialists can be hired to conduct risk.

Personal structural mitigation in earthquake prone areas include installation of an Earthquake Valve to instantly shut off the natural gas supply to your property, seismic retrofits of property and the securing of items inside the building to enhance household seismic safety such as the mounting of furniture, refrigerators, water heaters and breakables to the walls, and the addition of cabinet latches. In flood prone areas houses can be built on poles, like in much of southern Asia. In areas prone to prolonged electricity black-outs a generator would be an example of an optimal structural mitigation measure. The construction of storm cellars and fallout shelters are further examples of personal mitigative actions.

Preparedness

In the preparedness phase, emergency managers develop plans-of action for when the disaster strikes. Common preparedness measures include:

The Communication plans with easily understood terminology and chain of command.

Development and practice of multi-agency coordination and incident command.

Proper maintenance and training of emergency services.

Development and exercise of emergency population warning methods combined with emergency shelters and evacuation plans.

Stockpiling, inventory, and maintenance of supplies and equipment.

An efficient preparedness measure is an emergency operations centre (EOC) combined with a practiced region-wide doctrine for managing emergencies. Another preparedness measure is to develop a volunteer response capability among civilian populations. Since, volunteer response is not always as predictable and plan-able as professional response; volunteers are often deployed on the periphery of an emergency unless they are a proven and established volunteer organization with standards and training.

On the contrary to mitigation activities which are aimed at preventing a disaster from occurring, personal preparedness are targeted on preparing activities to be taken when a disaster occurs, *i.e.* planning. Preparedness measures can take many forms. Examples include the construction of shelters, warning devices, back-up life-line services (*e.g.* power, water, sewage), and rehearsing an evacuation plan. Two simple measures prepare you for either sitting out the event or evacuating. For evacuation, a disaster supplies kit should be prepared and for sheltering purposes a stockpile of supplies.

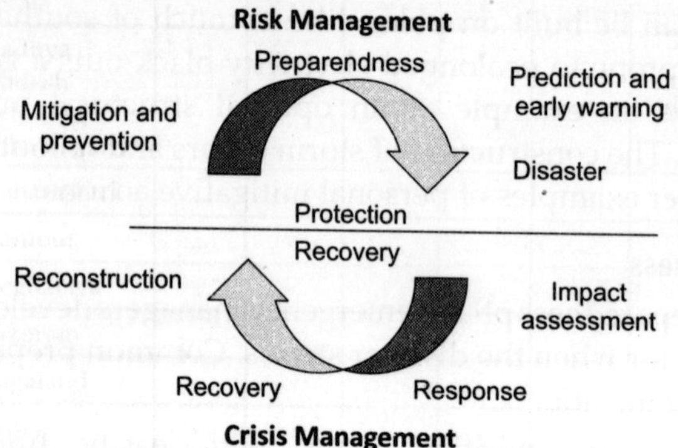

Response

The response phase includes the mobilization of the necessary emergency services and first responders in the disaster area. This is likely to include a first wave of core emergency services, such as fire-fighters, police and ambulance crews. They may be supported by a number of secondary emergency services, such as specialist rescue teams.

We work in all Phases of Disaster management and through our supported teams we respond in moments after a disaster hits as well as the other phases to try to reduce the chance of it happening in the first place or to reduce the impact of a disaster. We can respond worldwide to LEDCs (Less Economically Developed Countries) as well as MEDCs (More Economically Developed Countries).

In addition volunteers and other non-governmental organizations (NGOs) such as the local Red Cross branch or St. John Ambulance may provide immediate practical assistance, from first aid provision to providing tea and coffee. A well rehearsed emergency plan developed as part of the preparedness phase enables efficient coordination of rescue efforts. Emergency plan rehearsal is essential to achieve optimal output with limited resources. In the response phase, medical assets will be used in accordance with the appropriate triage of the affected victims.

A holistic and integrated approach will be evolved towards disaster management with emphasis on building strategic partnerships at various levels. The themes underpinning the policy are:

Community based DM, including last mile integration of the policy, plans and execution.

Capacity development in all spheres.

Consolidation of past initiatives and best practices.

Cooperation with agencies at national and international levels.

Multi-sectoral synergy.

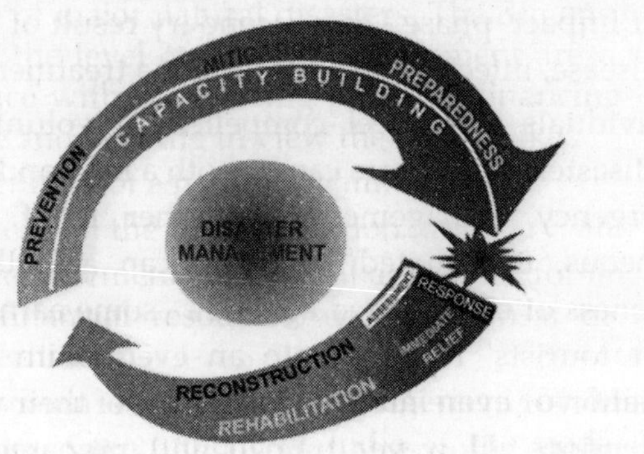

Survival Law of 3 S

Sometimes it is useful to remember the survival law of 3's is significant if you consider the survival profile of the person and the situation and add that to the other important factors in a survival situation. This works in a displaced wilderness scenario or a disaster, such as earthquakes in an urban or austere/mountainous environment:

Air 3 Minutes without air

Water 3 days without water

Food 3 weeks without food

Shelter Finding shelter is important to keep warm or cool and protected. (Some say 3 hours without shelter in harsh areas).

Health Proper healthy living, nutrition, activity, medical, etc., is needed.

Company / Moral: Some add - 3 months without companny.

Where required, search and rescue efforts commence at a very early stage. Depending on injuries sustained by the victim, outside temperature, and victim access to air and water, their location, etc., the vast majority of those severely affected by a disaster may die within 72 hours after impact. Within a week of a major incident SAR Teams often leave and the incident enters a 'Recovery phase'. Medical response obviously has obvious important applications in the 'Direct Impact' phase and the 'Indirect Impact' phase - as a secondary result of the incident. (Llike disease, infection and post-trauma treatment.)

Individuals often feel compelled to volunteer directly after a disaster. Volunteers can be both a help and a hindrance to emergency management and other relief agencies. A spontaneous, unaffiliated volunteer can actually harm the effectiveness of coordinated agencies - some earning the term 'disaster tourists' running into an event with preparation, coordination or even informing anyone - of their whereabouts and intentions. However trained and prepared volunteers under the direction of an organizing agency, such as mobile SAR Disaster Teams, can provide many benefits to the troubling effects of a disaster.

The response phase of an emergency may commence with a search and rescue phase. However in all cases the focus will be on fulfilling the basic needs of the affected population on a humanitarian basis. This assistance may be provided by national and/or international agencies and organisations. Effective coordination of disaster assistance is often crucial particularly when many organisations respond and Local Emergency Management Agency (LEMA) capacity may be over-stretched and diminished by the disaster itself.

On an individual or personal level, your decision / response can take the shape either of a home confinement or an evacuation. In a home confinement scenario a you and your family should be prepared to fend for yourselves in their home for several days without any form of outside support.

In an evacuation scenario, you and the family evacuates by a vehicle with the maximum amount of supplies, including a tent for shelter. The scenario could also include equipment for evacuation on foot with at least three days of supplies and rain-tight bedding a tarpaulin and a bedroll of blankets, would be the minimum.

Recovery

The aim of the recovery phase is to restore the affected area to its previous state. It differs from the response phase in its focus; recovery efforts are concerned with issues and decisions that must be made after immediate needs are addressed. Recovery efforts are primarily concerned with actions that involve rebuilding destroyed property, re-employment, and the repair of other essential infrastructure.

An important aspect of effective recovery efforts is taking advantage of a 'window of opportunity' for the implementation of mitigative measures that might otherwise be unpopular. Citizens of the affected area are more likely to accept more mitigative changes when a recent disaster is in fresh memory.

The recovery phase starts when the immediate threat to human life has subsided. In the reconstruction it is recommended to reconsider the location or construction material of the property.

In long-term disasters the most extreme home confinement scenarios like war, famine and severe epidemics last up to a year. In this situation the recovery will takeplace inside the home.

Planners for these events usually buy bulk foods and appropriate storage and preparation equipment, and eat the food as part of normal life. A simple balanced diet can be constructed from vitamin pills, whole-meal wheat, beans, dried milk, corn, and cooking oil. One should add vegetables, fruits, spices and meats, both prepared and fresh-gardened, when possible.

4 R'S of Rescue, Relief, Rehabilitation and Reconstruction

The standard timeframe of rescue, relief and rehabilitation are usually defined as approximately 7 days, 3 months and 5 years respectively. (This is an approximate rule.)

The rescue operation starts with the local residents, immediately after the earthquake/disaster. It is usually supported by the trained and skilled staffs from the (Urban) Search and Rescue (SAR) departments of the governments. These activities can be complemented by the non-government organizations (NGO).

International Relief Teams arrive in the later stage, usually after 24 hours, depending on the accessibility, and political relation with the country.

Rescue Phase

Rescue phase usually lasts for the first 48 to 72 hours after a disaster when the rate of survival of trapped victims is high. Rescue operations continue for much longer duration, however, after the first 2 to 3 day, the resources allocated for rescue are comparatively low since other priorities take over. Initially Rescue may be 'self-rescue' or the rescue by bystanders or witnesses.

Relief Phase

Relief phase followed immediately after the Rescue phase. During the relief phase, the focus is to provide basic necessities to victims of the earthquake and to restore social equilibrium. Detailed assessment of human and other losses is also usually carried out during the relief phase, which helps in optimal allocation of resources.

Relief phase may last between 1 to 3 months depending on the severity of the earthquake and the resources of the government. Community, supported by government is usually the central point. Added resources of the NGOs and the international organization substantiate this effort.

Rehabilitation / Reconstruction Phase Aims

Rehabilitation/reconstruction phase aims to restore the communities to the pre-earthquake status. During this phase, the social and other infrastructure is restored and economy revitalised. The rehabilitation/reconstruction phase typically starts at the end of relief phase and may last for several years.

The short-term plans of the recovery process are clearance of debris, building housing units, restoration of the lifelines and infrastructures, while the long-term objective is to build a safer and sustainable livelihood. Past experiences show that the efforts are sustainable only with community / government partnership, while NGOs and international organizations role is reduced after a certain period.

The Disaster Management Cycle: Therefore, disaster management can be divided in several phases, (depending on the perspective and definition of each phase).

Disaster Management Cycle

The Disaster management cycle illustrates the ongoing process by which governments, businesses, and civil society plan for and reduce the impact of disasters, react during and immediately following a disaster, and take steps to recover after a disaster has occurred. Appropriate actions at all points in the cycle lead to greater preparedness, better warnings, reduced vulnerability or the prevention of disasters during the next iteration of the cycle. The complete disaster management cycle includes the shaping of public policies and plans that either modify the causes of disasters or mitigate their effects on people, property, and infrastructure.

The disaster cycle or the disaster life cycle consists of the steps that emergency managers take in planning for and responding to disasters. Each step in the disaster cycle correlates to part of the ongoing cycle that is emergency management. This disaster cycle is used throughout the emergency management community, from the local to the national and international levels.

The first step of the disaster cycle is usually considered to be preparedness. Prior to a disaster's occurrence, emergency manager will plan for various disasters which could strike within the area of responsibility.

The second stage in the disaster cycle is response. Imminently prior to a disaster, warnings are issued and evacuations or sheltering in place occurs and necessary equipment is placed at the ready.

After the immediate response phase of the disaster cycle has been completed, the disaster turns toward recovery, focusing on the longer term response to the disaster. During the recovery phase of the disaster cycle, officials are interested in cleanup and rebuilding. During the recovery phase, lessons learned are collected and shared within the emergency response community.

The mitigation phase of the disaster cycle is almost concurrent with the recovery phase. The goal of the mitigation phase is to prevent the same disaster-caused damages from occurring again.

Finally, using the lessons learned from the response, recovery, and mitigation phases of the disaster the emergency manager and government officials return to the preparedness phase and revise their plans and their understanding of the material and human resources needs for a particular disaster in their community.

Disaster Management **Pages 133-152**
Edited by: Dr. Rabi Narayana Misra
ISBN: 978-93-88854-04-7
Edition: 2019
Published by: Discovery Publishing House Pvt. Ltd., New Delhi (India)

Disaster Management and its Emergency

[1]Dr. G. Chandnayya
[2]Dr. Rabi N. Misra

Introduction

Disaster management (or emergency management) is the creation of plans through which communities reduce vulnerability to hazards and cope with disasters. Disaster management does not avert or eliminate the threats; instead, it focuses on creating plans to decrease the effect of disasters. Failure to create a plan could lead to human mortality, lost revenue, and damage to assets. Events covered by disaster management include acts of terrorism, industrial sabotage, fire, natural disasters (such as earthquakes, hurricanes, etc.), public disorder, industrial accidents, and communication failures.

Emergency Planning Ideals

If possible, emergency planning should aim to prevent emergencies from occurring, and failing that, should develop a good action plan to mitigate the results and effects of any emergencies. As time goes on, and more data becomes available, usually through the study of emergencies as they occur, a plan should evolve. The development of emergency plans is a cyclical process, common to many risk management disciplines, such as Business Continuity and Security Risk Management, as set out below:

- Recognition or identification of risks.
- Ranking or evaluation of risks.

[1]Asst. Prof. Commerce, Govt. Degree Collage, Ravulapalem, A.P.
[2]Prof. MBA, SMIT, BPUT, Barhampur, Odisha.

- Responding to significant risks.
- Tolerate.
- Treat.
- Transfer.
- Terminate.
- Resourcing Controls.
- Reaction Planning.
- Reporting & monitoring risk performance.
- Reviewing the Risk Management framework.

There are a number of guidelines and publications regarding Emergency Planning, published by various professional organizations such as ASIS, National Fire Protection Association (NFPA), and the International Association of Emergency Managers (IAEM). There are very few Emergency Management specific standards, and emergency management as a discipline tends to fall under business resilience standards.

In order to avoid, or reduce significant losses to a business, emergency managers should work to identify and anticipate potential risks, hopefully to reduce their probability of occurring. In the event that an emergency does occur, managers should have a plan prepared to mitigate the effects of that emergency, as well as to ensure Business Continuity of critical operations post-incident. It is essential for an organisation to include procedures for determining whether an emergency situation has occurred and at what point an emergency management plan should be activated.

Implementation Ideate

This section does not cite any sources. Please help improve this section by adding citations to reliable sources. Unsourced material may be challenged and removed. (March 2014) (Learn how and when to remove this template message).

An emergency plan must be regularly maintained, in a structured and methodical manner, to ensure it is up-to-date in the event of an emergency. Emergency managers generally follow a common process to anticipate, assess, prevent, prepare, respond and recover from an incident.

Pre-incident Training and Testing

A team of emergency responders performs a training scenario involving anthrax.

Emergency management plans and procedures should include the identification of appropriately trained staff members responsible for decision-making when an emergency occurs. Training plans should include internal people, contractors and civil protection partners, and should state the nature and frequency of training and testing.

Testing of a plan's effectiveness should occur regularly. In instances where several business or organisations occupy the same space, joint emergency plans, formally agreed to by all parties, should be put into place.

Communicating and Incident Assessment

Communication is one of the key issues during any emergency, pre-planning of communications is critical. Miscommunication can easily result in emergency events escalating unnecessarily.

Once an emergency has been identified a comprehensive assessment evaluating the level of impact and its financial implications should be undertaken. Following assessment, the appropriate plan or response to be activated will depend on a specific pre-set criteria within the emergency plan. The steps necessary should be prioritized to ensure critical functions are operational as soon as possible. The critical functions are those that makes the plan untenable if not operationalized.

The Communication policy must be well known and rehearsed and all targeted audiences or publics and individuals must be alert. All Communication infrastructure must be as prepared as possible with all information on groupings clearly identified.

Phases and Personal Activities

This section needs additional citations for verification. Please help improve this article by adding citations to reliable sources. Unsourced material may be challenged and removed. (March 2014) (Learn how and when to remove this template message)

Emergency management consists of five phases: *prevention, mitigation, preparedness, response and recovery.*

Prevention

It focuses on preventing the human hazard, primarily from potential natural disasters or terrorist attacks. Preventive measures are taken on both the domestic and international levels, designed to provide permanent protection from disasters. Not all disasters, particularly natural disasters, can be prevented, but the risk of loss of life and injury can be mitigated with good evacuation plans, environmental planning and design standards. In January 2005, 167 Governments adopted a 10-year global plan for natural disaster risk reduction called the Hyogo Framework.[citation needed]

Preventing or reducing the impacts of disasters on our communities is a key focus for emergency management efforts today. Prevention and mitigation also help reduce the financial costs of disaster response and recovery. Public Safety Canada is working with provincial and territorial governments and stakeholders to promote disaster prevention and mitigation using a risk-based and all-hazards approach. In 2008, Federal/Provincial/Territorial Ministers endorsed a National Disaster Mitigation Strategy.

Mitigation

Preventive or mitigation measures take different forms for different types of disasters. In earthquake prone areas, these preventive measures might include structural changes such as the installation of an earthquake valve to instantly shut off the natural gas supply, seismic retrofits of property, and the securing of items inside a building. The latter may include the mounting of furniture, refrigerators, water heaters and breakables to the walls, and the addition of cabinet latches. In flood prone areas, houses can be built on poles/stilts. In areas prone to prolonged electricity black-outs installation of a generator ensures continuation of electrical service. The construction of storm cellars and fallout shelters are further examples of personal mitigative actions.

On a national level, governments might implement large scale mitigation measures. After the monsoon floods of 2010, the Punjab government subsequently constructed 22 'disaster-resilient' model villages, comprising 1885 single-storey homes, together with schools and health centres.

Disaster mitigation measures are those that eliminate or reduce the impacts and risks of hazards through proactive measures taken before an emergency or disaster occurs.

One of the best known examples of investment in disaster mitigation is the Red River Floodway. The building of the Floodway was a joint provincial/federal undertaking to protect the City of Winnipeg and reduce the impact of flooding in the Red River Basin. It cost $62.7 million to build in the 1960s. Since then, the floodway has been used over 20 times. Its use during the 1997 Red River Flood alone saved an estimated $4.5 billion in costs from potential damage to the city. The Floodway was expanded in 2006 as a joint provincial/federal initiative.

Preparedness

An airport emergency preparedness exercise.

Preparedness focuses on preparing equipment and procedures for use when a disaster occurs. This equipment and these procedures can be used to reduce vulnerability to disaster, to mitigate the impacts of a disaster or to respond more efficiently in an emergency. The Federal Emergency Management Agency (FEMA) has set out a basic four-stage vision of preparedness flowing from mitigation to preparedness to response to recovery and back to mitigation in a circular planning process. This circular, overlapping model has been modified by other agencies, taught in emergency class and discussed in academic papers. FEMA also operates a Building Science Branch that develops and produces multi-hazard mitigation guidance that focuses on creating disaster-resilient communities to reduce loss of life and property. FEMA advises citizens to prepare their homes with some emergency essentials in the case that the food distribution lines are interrupted. FEMA has subsequently prepared for this contingency by purchasing hundreds of thousands of freeze dried food emergency meals ready to eat (MRE's) to dispense to the communities where emergency shelter and evacuations are implemented.

Some guidelines for household preparedness have been put on line by the State of Colorado, on the topics of water, food, tools, and so on.

Emergency preparedness can be difficult to measure. CDC focuses on evaluating the effectiveness of its public health efforts through a variety of measurement and assessment programmes.

Local Emergency Planning Committees

Local Emergency Planning Committees (LEPCs) are required by the United States Environmental Protection Agency under the Emergency Planning and Community Right-to-Know Act to develop an emergency response plan, review the plan at least annually, and provide information about chemicals in the community to local citizens. This emergency preparedness effort focuses on hazards presented by use and storage of extremely hazardous, hazardous and toxic chemicals.Particular requirements of LEPCs include:

- Identification of facilities and transportation routes of extremely hazardous substances.
- Description of emergency response procedures, on and off site.
- Designation of a community coordinator and facility emergency coordinator(s) to implement the plan.
- Outline of emergency notification procedures.
- Description of how to determine the probable affected area and population by releases.
- Description of local emergency equipment and facilities and the persons responsible for them.
- Outline of evacuation plans.
- A training programme for emergency responders (including schedules).

- Methods and schedules for exercising emergency response plans.

According to the EPA, "Many LEPCs have expanded their activities beyond the requirements of EPCRA, encouraging accident prevention and risk reduction, and addressing homeland security in their communities" and the Agency offers advice on how to evaluate the effectiveness of these committees.

Preparedness Measures

Preparedness measures can take many forms ranging from focusing on individual people, locations or incidents to broader, government-based "all hazard" planning. [14] There are a number of preparedness stages between "all hazard' and individual planning, generally involving some combination of both mitigation and response planning. Business continuity planning encourages businesses to have a Disaster Recovery Plan. Community- and faith- based organizations mitigation efforts promote field response teams and inter-agency planning.

Classroom Response Kit

School-based response teams cover everything from live shooters to gas leaks and nearby bank robberies. Educational institutions plan for cyberattacks and windstorms.Industry specific guidance exists for horse farms, boat owners and more.

Family preparedness for disaster is fairly unusual. A 2013 survey found that only 19% of American families felt that they were "very prepared" for a disaster. Still, there are many resources available for family disaster planning. The Department of Homeland Security's Ready.gov page includes a Family Emergency Plan Checklist, has a whole webpage devoted to readiness for kids, complete with cartoon-style superheroes, and ran a Thunderclap Campaign in 2014. The Center for Disease Control has a Zombie Apocalypse website.

Kitchen Fire Extinguisher

Disasters take a variety of forms to include earthquakes, tsunamis or regular structure fires. That a disaster or emergency is not large scale in terms of population or acreage impacted or duration does not make it any less of a disaster for the people or area impacted and much can be learned about preparedness from so-called small disasters. The Red Cross states that it responds to nearly 70,000 disasters a year, the most common of which is a single family fire.

Items on Shelves in Basement

Preparedness starts with an individual's everyday life and involves items and training that would be useful in an emergency. What is useful in an emergency is often also useful in everyday life. From personal preparedness, preparedness continues on a continuum through family preparedness, community preparedness and then business, non-profit and governmental preparedness. Some organizations blend these various levels. For example, the International Red Cross and Red Crescent Movement has a webpage on disaster training as well as offering training on basic preparedness such as Cardiopulmonary resuscitation and First Aid. Other non-profits such as Team Rubicon bring specific groups of people into disaster preparedness and response operations. FEMA breaks down preparedness into a pyramid, with citizens on the foundational bottom, on top of which rests local government, state government and federal government in that order.

Non-Perishable Food in Cabinet

The basic theme behind preparedness is to be ready for an emergency and there are a number of different variations of being ready based on an assessment of what sort of threats exist. Nonetheless, there is basic guidance for preparedness that is common despite an area's specific dangers. FEMA recommends that everyone have a three-day survival kit for their household. Because individual household sizes and specific needs might vary, FEMA's recommendations are not item specific, but the list includes:

- Three-day supply of non-perishable food.
- Three-day supply of water - one gallon of water per person, per day.

- Portable, battery-powered radio or television and extra batteries.
- Flashlight and extra batteries.
- First aid kit and manual.
- Sanitation and hygiene items (*e.g.* toilet paper, menstrual hygiene products).
- Matches and waterproof container.
- Whistle.
- Extra clothing.
- Kitchen accessories and cooking utensils, including a can opener.
- Photocopies of credit and identification cards.
- Cash and coins.
- Special needs items, such as prescription medications, eyeglasses, contact lens solutions, and hearing aid batteries.
- Items for infants, such as formula, diapers, bottles, and pacifiers.
- Other items to meet unique family needs.
- Along similar lines, but not exactly the same, CDC has its own list for a proper disaster supply kit.
- Water—one gallon per person, per day.
- Food—nonperishable, easy-to-prepare items.
- Flashlight.
- Battery powered or hand crank radio (IMOAA Weather Radio, if possible).
- Extra batteries.
- First aid kit.
- Medications (7-day supply), other medical supplies, and medical paperwork (*e.g.*, medication list and pertinent medical information).
- Multipurpose tool (*e.g.*, Swiss army knife).
- Sanitation and personal hygiene items.

- Copies of personal documents (*e.g.*, proof of address, deed/lease to home, passports, birth certificates, and insurance policies).
- Cell phone with chargers.
- Family and emergency contact information.
- Extra cash.
- Emergency blanket.
- Map(s) of the area.
- Extra set of car keys and house keys.
- Manual can opener.

Children are a special population when considering Emergency preparedness and many resources are directly focused on supporting them. SAMHSA has list of tips for talking to children during infectious disease outbreaks, to include being a good listener, encouraging children to ask questions and modeling self-care by setting routines, eating healthy meals, getting enough sleep and taking deep breaths to handle stress. [33] FEMA has similar advice, noting that "Disasters can leave children feeling frightened, confused, and insecure" whether a child has experienced it first hand, had it happen to a friend or simply saw it on television. In the same publication, FEMA further notes, "Preparing for disaster helps everyone in the family accept the fact that disasters do happen, and provides an opportunity to identify and collect the resources needed to meet basic needs after disaster. Preparation helps; when people feel prepared, they cope better and so do children."

To help people assess what threats might be in order to augment their emergency supplies or improve their disaster response skills, FEMA has published a booklet called the "Threat and Hazard Identification and Risk Assessment Guide." (THIRA) This guide, which outlines the THIRA process, emphasizes "whole community involvement," not just governmental agencies, in preparedness efforts. In this guide, FEMA breaks down hazards into three categories: Natural, technological and human caused and notes that each hazard should be assessed for both its likelihood and its significance. According to FEMA, "Communities should consider only those threats and hazards that could plausibly occur" and "Communities should consider only those threats and hazards that would have a significant effect on them." To develop threat and hazard context descriptions, communities should take into account the time, place, and conditions in which threats or hazards might occur.

Not all preparedness efforts and discussions involve the government or established NGOs like the Red Cross. Emergency preparation discussions are active on the internet, with many blogs and websites dedicated to discussing various aspects of preparedness. On-line sales of items such as survival food, medical supplies and heirloom seeds allow people to stock basements with cases of food and drinks with 25 year shelf lives, sophisticated medical kits and seeds that are guaranteed to sprout even after years of storage.

One group of people who put a lot of effort in disaster preparations is called Doomsday Preppers. This subset of preparedness-minded people often share a belief that the FEMA or Red Cross emergency preparation suggestions and training are not extensive enough. Sometimes called survivalists, Doomsday Preppers are often preparing for The End Of The World As We Know It, abbreviated as TEOTWAWKI. With a motto some have that "The Future Belongs to those who Prepare," this Preparedness subset has its own set of Murphy's Rules, including "Rule Number 1: Food, you still don't have enough" and "Rule Number 26: People who thought the Government would save them, found out that it didn't."

Not all emergency preparation efforts revolve around food, guns and shelters, though these items help address the needs in the bottom two sections of Maslow's hierarchy of needs. The American Preppers Network has an extensive list of items that might be useful in less apparent ways than a first aid kid or help add 'fun' to challenging times. These items include:

- Books and magazines.
- Arts and crafts painting.
- Children's entertainment.

- Crayons and coloring books.
- Notebooks and writing supplies.
- Nuts, bolts, screws, nails, etc.
- Religious material.
- Sporting equipment, card games and board games.
- Posters and banners creating awareness.

Emergency preparedness goes beyond immediate family members. For many people, pets are an integral part of their families and emergency preparation advice includes them as well. It is not unknown for pet owners to die while trying to rescue their pets from a fire or from drowning. CDC's Disaster Supply Checklist for Pets includes:

- Food and water for at least 3 days for each pet; bowls, and a manual can opener.
- Depending on the pet you may need a litter box, paper towels, plastic trash bags, grooming items, and/or household bleach.
- Medications and medical records stored in a waterproof container.
- First aid kit with a pet first aid book.
- Sturdy leash, harness, and carrier to transport pet safely. A carrier should be large enough for the animal to stand comfortably, turn around, and lie down. Your pet may have to stay in the carrier for several hours.
- Pet toys and the pet's bed, if you can easily take it, to reduce stress.
- Current photos and descriptions of your pets to help others identify them in case you and your pets become separated, and to prove that they are yours.
- Information on feeding schedules, medical conditions, behaviour problems, and the name and telephone number of your veterinarian in case you have to board your pets or place them in foster care.

Emergency preparedness also includes more than physical items and skill-specific training. Psychological preparedness is also a type of emergency preparedness and specific mental health preparedness resources are offered for mental health professionals by organizations such as the Red Cross. These mental health preparedness resources are designed to support both community members affected by a disaster and the disaster workers serving them. CDC has a website devoted to coping with a disaster or traumatic event. After such an event, the CDC, through the Substance Abuse and Mental Health Services Administration (SAMHSA), suggests that people seek psychological help when they exhibit symptoms such as excessive worry, crying frequently, an increase in irritability, anger, and frequent arguing, wanting to be alone most of the time, feeling anxious or fearful, overwhelmed by sadness, confused, having trouble thinking clearly and concentrating, and difficulty making decisions, increased alcohol and/or substance use, increased physical (aches, pains) complaints such as headaches and trouble with "nerves."

Sometimes emergency supplies are kept in what is called a Bug-out bag. While FEMA does not actually use the term "Bug out bag," calling it instead some variation of a "Go Kit," the idea of having emergency items in a quickly accessible place is common to both FEMA and CDC, though on-line discussions of what items a "bug out bag" should include sometimes cover items such as firearms and great knives that are not specifically suggested by FEMA or CDC. The theory behind a "bug out bag" is that emergency preparations should include the possibility of Emergency evacuation. Whether fleeing a burning building or hastily packing a car to escape an impending hurricane, flood or dangerous chemical release, rapid departure from a home or workplace environment is always a possibility and FEMA suggests having a Family Emergency Plan for such occasions. Because family members may not be together when disaster strikes, this plan should include reliable contact information for friends or relatives who live outside of what would be the disaster area for household members to notify they are safe or otherwise communicate with each other. Along with the contact information, FEMA suggests having well-understood local gathering points if a house must be evacuated quickly to avoid the dangers of re-reentering a burning home. Family and emergency contact information should be printed on cards and put in each family member's backpack or wallet. If family members spend a significant amount of time in a specific location, such as at work or school, FEMA suggests learning the emergency preparation plans for those places. FEMA has a specific form, in English and in Spanish, to help people put together these emergency plans, though it lacks lines for email contact information.

Like children, people with disabilities and other special needs have special emergency preparation needs. While "disability" has a specific meaning for specific organizations such as collecting Social Security benefits for the purposes of emergency preparedness, the Red Cross uses the term in a broader sense to include people with physical, medical, sensor or cognitive disabilities or the elderly and other special needs populations.[45] Depending on the particular disability, specific emergency preparations might be required. FEMA's suggestions for people with disabilities includes having copies of prescriptions, charging devices for medical devices such as motorized wheel chairs and a week's supply of medication readily available LINK or in a "go stay kit." In some instances, lack of competency in English may lead to special preparation requirements and communication efforts for both individuals and responders.

FEMA notes that long-term power outages can cause damage beyond the original disaster that can be mitigated with emergency generators or other power sources to provide an Emergency power system. The United States Department of Energy states that 'homeowners, business owners, and local leaders may have to take an active role in dealing with energy disruptions on their own." This active role may include installing or other procuring generators that are either portable or permanently mounted and run on fuels such as propane or natural gas or gasoline. Concerns about carbon monoxide poisoning, electrocution, flooding, fuel storage and fire lead even small property owners to consider professional installation and maintenance. Major institutions like hospitals, military bases and educational institutions often have or are considering extensive backup power systems. Instead of, or in addition to, fuel-based power systems, solar, wind and other alternative power sources may be used. Standalone batteries, large or small, are also used to provide backup charging for electrical systems and devices ranging from emergency lights to computers to cell phones.

Emergency preparedness does not stop at home or at school. The United States Department of Health and Human Services addresses specific emergency preparedness issues hospitals may have to respond to, including maintaining a safe temperature, providing adequate electricity for life support systems and even carrying out evacuations under extreme circumstances. FEMA encourages all businesses to have businesses to have an emergency response plan and the Small Business Administration specifically advises small business owners to also focus emergency preparedness and provides a variety of different worksheets and resources.

FEMA cautions that emergencies happen while people are travelling as well and provides guidance around emergency preparedness for a range travelers to include commuters,[60] Commuter Emergency Plan and holiday travelers. In particular, Ready.gov has a number of emergency preparations specifically designed for people with cars. These preparations include having a full gas tank, maintaining adequate windshield wiper fluid and other basic car maintenance tips. Items specific to an emergency include:

- Jumper cables: might want to include flares or reflective triangle.
- Flashlights, to include extra batteries (batteries have less power in colder weather).
- First Aid Kit, to include any necessary medications, baby formula and diapers if caring for small children.

- Non-perishable food such as canned food (be alert to liquids freezing in colder weather), and protein rich foods like nuts and energy bars.
- Manual can opener.
- At least 1 gallon of water per person a day for at least 3 days (be alert to hazards of frozen water and resultant container rupture).
- *Basic tool kit:* pliers, wrench, screwdriver.
- *Pet supplies:* food and water.
- *Radio:* battery or hand cranked.
- *For snowy areas:* cat litter or sand for better tire traction; shovel; ice scraper; warm clothes, gloves, hat, sturdy boots, jacket and an extra change of clothes.
- Blankets or sleeping bags.
- *Charged Cell Phone:* and car charger.

In addition to emergency supplies and training for various situations, FEMA offers advice on how to mitigate disasters. The Agency gives instructions on how to retrofit a home to minimize hazards from a Flood, to include installing a Backflow prevention device, anchoring fuel tanks and relocating electrical panels.

Marked Gas Shuttoff

Given the explosive danger posed by natural gas leaks, Ready.gov states unequivocally that "It is vital that all household members know how to shut off natural gas" and that property owners must ensure they have any special tools needed for their particular gas hookups. Ready.gov also notes that "It is wise to teach all responsible household members where and how to shut off the electricity," cautioning that individual circuits should be shut off before the main circuit. Ready.gov further states that "It is vital that all household members learn how to shut off the water at the main house valve" and cautions that the possibility that rusty valves might require replacement.

Response

The response phase of an emergency may commence with Search and Rescue but in all cases the focus will quickly

turn to fulfilling the basic humanitarian needs of the affected population. This assistance may be provided by national or international agencies and organizations. Effective coordination of disaster assistance is often crucial, particularly when many organizations respond and local emergency management agency (LEMA) capacity has been exceeded by the demand or diminished by the disaster itself. The National Response Framework is a United States government publication that explains responsibilities and expectations of government officials at the local, state, federal, and tribal levels. It provides guidance on Emergency Support Functions that may be integrated in whole or parts to aid in the response and recovery process.

On a personal level the response can take the shape either of a shelter in place or an evacuation.

Evacuation Sign

In a shelter-in-place scenario, a family would be prepared to fend for themselves in their home for many days without any form of outside support. In an evacuation, a family leaves the area by automobile or other mode of transportation, taking with them the maximum amount of supplies they can carry, possibly including a tent for shelter. If mechanical transportation is not available, evacuation on foot would ideally include carrying at least three days of supplies and rain-tight bedding, a tarpaulin and a bedroll of blankets.

Donations are often sought during this period, especially for large disasters that overwhelm local capacity. Due to efficiencies of scale, money is often the most cost-effective donation if fraud is avoided. Money is also the most flexible, and if goods are sourced locally then transportation is minimized and the local economy is boosted. Some donors prefer to send gifts in kind, however these items can end up creating issues, rather than helping. One innovation by Occupy Sandy volunteers is to use a donation registry, where families and businesses impacted by the disaster can make specific requests, which remote donors can purchase directly via a web site.

Medical considerations will vary greatly based on the type of disaster and secondary effects. Survivors may sustain a multitude of injuries to include lacerations, burns, near drowning, or crush syndrome.

Recovery

The recovery phase starts after the immediate threat to human life has subsided. The immediate goal of the recovery phase is to bring the affected area back to normalcy as quickly as possible. During reconstruction it is recommended to consider the location or construction material of the property.

The most extreme home confinement scenarios include war, famine and severe epidemics and may last a year or more. Then recovery will take place inside the home. Planners for these events usually buy bulk foods and appropriate storage and preparation equipment, and eat the food as part of normal life. A simple balanced diet can be constructed from vitamin pills, whole-meal wheat, beans, dried milk, corn, and cooking oil.[65] One should add vegetables, fruits, spices and meats, both prepared and fresh-gardened, when possible.

As a Profession

This section needs additional citations for verification. Please help improve this article by adding citations to reliable sources. Unsourced material may be challenged and removed. (March 2014) (Learn how and when to remove this template message)

Professional emergency managers can focus on government and community preparedness, or private business preparedness. Training is provided by local, state, federal and private organizations and ranges from public information and media relations to high-level incident command and tactical skills.

In the past, the field of emergency management has been populated mostly by people with a military or first responder background. Currently, the field has become more diverse, with many managers coming from a variety of backgrounds other than the military or first responder fields. Educational opportunities are increasing for those seeking undergraduate and graduate degrees in emergency management or a related field. There are over 180 schools in the US with emergency management-related programmes, but only one doctoral programme specifically in emergency management.

Professional certifications such as Certified Emergency Manager (CEM) and Certified Business Continuity Professional (CBCP) are becoming more common as professional standards are raised throughout the field, particularly in the United States. There are also professional organizations for emergency managers, such as the National Emergency Management Association and the International Association of Emergency Managers.

Principles

In 2007, Dr. Wayne Blanchard of FEMA's Emergency Management Higher Education Project, at the direction of Dr. Cortez Lawrence, Superintendent of FEMA's Emergency Management Institute, convened a working group of emergency management practitioners and academics to consider principles of emergency management. This was the first time the principles of the discipline were to be codified. The group agreed on eight principles that will be used to guide the development of a doctrine of emergency management.

Conclusions

1. Comprehensive - consider and take into account all hazards, all phases, all stakeholders and all impacts relevant to disasters.
2. Progressive - anticipate future disasters and take preventive and preparatory measures to build disaster-resistant and disaster-resilient communities.
3. Risk-driven - use sound risk management principles (hazard identification, risk analysis, and impact analysis) in assigning priorities and resources.
4. Integrated - ensure unity of effort among all levels of government and all elements of a community.
5. Collaborative - create and sustain broad and sincere relationships among individuals and organizations to encourage trust, advocate a team atmosphere, build consensus, and facilitate communication.

6. Coordinated - synchronize the activities of all relevant stakeholders to achieve a common purpose.
7. Flexible - use creative and innovative approaches in solving disaster challenges.
8. Professional - value a science and knowledge-based approach; based on education, training, experience, ethical practice, public stewardship and continuous improvement.

In recent years the continuity feature of emergency management has resulted in a new concept, Emergency Management Information Systems (EMIS). For continuity and interoperability between emergency management stakeholders, EMIS supports an infrastructure that integrates emergency plans at all levels of government and non-government involvement for all four phases of emergencies. In the healthcare field, hospitals utilize the Hospital Incident Command System (HICS), which provides structure and organization in a clearly defined chain of command. [citation needed]

Disaster Management **Pages 153-162**
Edited by: Dr. Rabi Narayana Misra
ISBN: 978-93-88854-04-7
Edition: 2019
Published by: Discovery Publishing House Pvt. Ltd., New Delhi (India)

Chapter 12

Managing Disaster

An unavoidable Hazard—A Study

[1]Dr. Prafulla Chandra Mohanty

Introduction

Disaster is an event which is generally unpredictable, happens instantly without giving enough time to react, affecting a large number of people, disrupting normal life and leading to a large scale devastation in terms of loss of life and property, always finding the administration and affected people struggling to respond in the desired manner and leaving deep socio-psychological, political and economic after effects which persist for a long time to come. United Nations defined "disaster as a serious disruption of the functioning of a community or a society. Disasters involve widespread human, material, economic or environmental impacts, which exceed the ability of the affected community or society to cope using its own resources". Similarly, the Red Cross and Red Crescent societies define disaster management as the organization and management of resources and responsibilities for dealing with all humanitarian aspects of emergencies, in particular preparedness, response and recovery in order to lessen the impact of disasters. The Concise Oxford Dictionary defines disaster as "A sudden or great misfortune a calamity". Disaster generally mean any type of chemical biological reactions, costal storm, contaminated water born diseases; dam leavy break, drought, earthquake, emergency planning, explosions, extreme temperature, fire, flooding, hurricane, industrial hardship,

[1]Retd. Principal, Resident At-Sanskruti Sadan, Bayali, Mantridi, Dist-Ganjam, State-Odisha, PIN-761008.

mudslide and landslide, radiation leak, severe storms, snow storms, straight line winds, technological hazards, terrorism, declared and undeclared wars, typhoon, virus threat, volcano, wildfire, winter storm and different modern electronically, and electrical, nuclear and scientific hazards, etc. The paper studies especially on different concepts, analyses in tables regarding the disasters of the World and of India it also gives some preventive measures to mitigate the human and material losses. At the end the study leaves some suggestions for policy maker with a conclusion.

Types of Disasters

These felt disasters mainly are of four types. They are like Natural disaster, Environmental emergencies, complex emergency and pandemic emergencies. Natural disasters are occurred naturally and they include floods, hurricanes, earthquakes, hail storm rains and volcano eruptions that have immediate impacts on human health and then impacts causing further death and suffering from floods, landslides, fires, tsunamis etc. Environmental disasters are technological or industrial accidents, usually involving the production, use or transportation of hazardous material, and occur where these materials are produced, used or transported, and forest fires caused by humans.

Complex emergencies are like the involving a break-down of authority, looting and attacks on strategic installations, including conflict situations and war. Similarly Pandemic emergencies are sudden onset of contagious disease that affects health, disrupts services and businesses, brings economic and social costs.

Effect of Disasters

Any disaster can interrupt essential services, such as health care, electricity, water, sewage (garbage) removal, transportation and communications. The interruption can seriously affect the health, social and economic networks of local communities and countries. Disasters have a major and long lasting impact on people long after immediate effect have been mitigated. Poorly planned relief activities can have a significant negative impact not only on the disaster victims but also on donors and relief agencies. So it is important that Physical Therapist join established programmes rather than attempting individual efforts. Local, regional, national and international organzation are all involved in mounting and humanitarian response to disasters. Each will nave a prepfared disaster management plan. These plans cover mostly the prevention, preparedness, relief and recovery works. Disasters may also be classified as natural. man-made and human induced. Disaster occurred in varied forms like Predictable disasters in advance, some others are annual or seasonal and others are sudden and unpredictable. The disasters are also of materiological, geological, ecological or environmental, technological disasters. Natural disasters are again be classified into some sub-groups like earthquakes, floods, cyclones, droughts, landslides, pest attacks, forest fires, avalanches etc.

Consequences and Causes of Disaster

Generally the disaster bring several types of irreparable losses like- loss of human lives, diseases, disabilities, distresses, dislocations and disorganization in the human, plant, animal and also in material world. Disasters create starvation, loss of water and power supply, unemployment, destruction of roads, rails and other ways of communications. The disasters may be of physical, psychological and of socio-economical. The physical disasters are of fractures, burns, injuries, infections, poisoning. Similarly the Psychological disasters are like depression, grief, anger, guilt, apathy, fear, the 'burnout' syndrome, suicide, bizarre behaviour, bereavement, anxiety, alcohol abuse, stress and other mental and psychological reactions. Similarly the socio-economic effect of disasters include environmental destruction, unemployment, disorganization and homelessness. Some other examples of environmental disasters are - global warming, depletion of ozen layer, solar fire etc. Industrial accidents, transport accidents/chemical and nuclear power accidents are common hazards coming under industrial and technical disasters. There are also some dangerous man-made disasters like war, looting, social and religious conflicts, bomb-blasting, stampedes during congregation. Pandemic disasters like bird flue, plague and other kind of serious epidemic viral diseases bring a lot of irreparable losses to human and animal societies. No disaster will occur for no cause. So every disaster must have a cause. The environmental scientists have elaborated some causes of these disasters like increased urbanization, over population, degradation in the natural environment, human stupidity and carelessness.

World and Disasters

The human loss and damages by disaster are enumerated by the following Tables which are based on World Disaster Report 2014.

Human Loss by World Disasters

Types of Disaster	No. of Disasters in 2013	Total No. of Disasters during 2004-13	Human loss In 2013 Disasters	Human loss during 2004-13	Avg. Human loss per year
Draught/Food Insecurity	12	225	NA	384	38.4
Earthquakes/ Tsunamis	28	269	1120	650321	65032.1
Extreme Temperature	17	264	1962	72088	7208.8
Floods/waves/ surges	149	752	9819	63207	6320.7
Forest/scrubtrees	10	94	35	705	70.5
Insect infestation	NDR	14	NDR	NA	NA
Mass movement (Dry)	01	08	46	273	27.3
Mass movement (Wet)	11	173	235	8739	873.9

Volcanic Eruptions	03	57	NA	363	36.3
Windstorms	106	1011	9215	183457	18345.7
Subtotal: Hydro-meteorological Disasters	305	3533	21286	328580	32858.0
Sub-total: Physical Disasters	32	334	1166	650957	65095.7
Total Natural Disassters	337	3867	22452	979537	97953.7
Industrial Accidents	25	473	1907	13750	1375.0
Miscellaneous Accidents	31	399	1003	13002	1300.2
Transport Accidents	136	1786	3801	52783	5278.3
Total Technological Disasters	192	2658	6711	79535	7953.5
Total	529	6525	29163	1059072	105907.2

Source : EM-DAT, CRED, University of Lounch, Belgium.

Note: Total No of people reported killed by type:

- Includes waves and surges.
- Landslides, rock falls, subsidence etc. of geophysical origin.
- Landslides, avalanches, subsidence etc. of hydrological origin.

Sum totals in this Table may not correspond due to rounding up, NDA signifies no data available and n.d.r. no disaster reported. In 2013, the number of people killed by natural disasters was at their fourth lowest level of the decade, as was the number of deaths from windstorms. (41 per cent in 2013 versus a 19 per cent average for the decade) However, deaths caused by earthquakes represented only 5 per cent of total death against a 67 per cent average for the decade. The two deadliest natural disaster in 2013 were Typhoon Halyan in the Philippines (7,986 deaths) and monsoonal flood in India (6054 deaths). The major disasters of the decade were the Indian Ocean Tsunami in 2004 (226, 408 deaths), the Haiti earthquake in 2010 (222,570 deaths); Cyclone Nargis in Myanmar in 2008 (138,375 deaths), the Sichuan earthquake in China in 2008 (87,478 deaths) the 2005 Kashmir earthquake (74648 deaths), and a heat wave in Russia in 2010 (55,736 deaths).

Damages by World Disasters

(in million US Dollar)

Continet	Damages in 2013 Disaster in million US Dollar	Decadal damages during 2004-13 Disaster	Avg. damages per year in million US Dollars
Africa	241	6783	678.3
America	34770	710415	71042
Asia	58521	759674	75967.4
Europe	22427	139419	13941.9
Oceania	3259	53338	5333.8
Very high human development	52124	1119023	111902.3
High human development	9041	95138	9513.8
Medium human development	58255	404090	40409.0
Low human development	01788	51374	5137.4
Total	119217	1659626	165962.6

Source: EM DAT, CRED, University of Launch, Belgium.

Note : Score totals in the Table may not correspond due to roundingup.

The total amount of damage reported in 2013 was the fourth lowest of the decade. It was also the fourth lowest in Africa and the America. But it was the fourth highest in Asia and the 3rd highest in Europe and Oceania. However, in Asia and Oceania the amount of damages retained below their average for decade. The amount of damages were the 3rd lowest in very high and low human development countries. Out of the highest in high human development countries and the 3rd highest in those of the medium development. The contribution of Europe to the total amount of damages climbed to 19% for higher than their 8% average for the decade. On the other hand the contribution of the America in 2013 (29%) was largely below its average for the decade (43%). Asia acounted for 49% of the reported damages, slightly above its average for the decade (46%) contributions of Oceania (3%) and Africa (0.2%) where lower than their respective 3.2 and 0.4% average for the decade. The highest contribution to the damages (47%) came from medium human development countries, for above their 24% average for the decade. Disaster damages in very high human development countries aounted for 44% of total damages, a much lower percentage than their 67% average for the decade.

India and Disasters

Whole of the Indian Peninsula is under disaster prone area. A survey reports that 68 per cent of our Indian Land are prone to draught, 50 per cent of the area to earthquake, 12 per cent to flood and 8 per cent towards cyclone. Mostly Assam, Bihar, Odisha, Uttar Pradesh and West Bengal are the areas affected seriously by floods. Rajasthan, Gujrat, Bihar and a part of Odisha are prone to draught. 40 million hectres of these states are affected invariably to draught. North-East and North-West states are exhibiting the disasters like landslides. Similarly the rural areas of North India are affected by cold waves. In India, the annual impact of disasters is 4334 numbers of loss in lives, more than 30 million people are affected by these disasters and at about 2.34 million houses are lost. It is seen from the data that in 1991-95, the economic losses are 36000 crores of rupees during 1996-2000 the losses increased by another 50 per cent and reached to 54,000 crores and similarly in 2001 - 2005 the loss grew by 139 per cent and reached to 86,000 crores. For rehabilitation and other fellowup activities, the country faced an average central revenue loss of not less than 12 per cent on relief leaving aside the loss sustained by state government. It was seen from the www.em-dat.net. That UNO declared the decade of 1990-1999 as International Decade for Natural Disaster Reduction. This observation is for creating Universal awareness to reduce losses on disaster. During the year 1995-1999- the losses from disaster of Developed World was 2.5% of the GDP, whereas in the developing world the said loss was 13.4% of the GDP. The total loss of the globe estimated an year was about 700 U.S. billion dollars. Some of the worst affectad disasters in the history of India: The great Bengal Famine in Bengal during the British rule in the period of 1769-1773. Bengal Famine was caused the deaths of 10 million people in Bengal, Bihar and of Odisha. The Coringa Cyclone was one of the 10 big disasters that shock India struck at a tiny village of Godavari district in Andhra Pradesh. The Great Coringa Cyclone killed around 20,000 people in the ancient city of Coringa in 1839. In 1896, the major plague pandemic came to British India killing more than 12 million people in India and China alone. The plague pandemic was initially seen in port cities of Bombay and Kolkata, then spread to small towns and rural areas of India. In 1979 Lahaul Valley Avalanche (snowfall) in March of 1979 which buried 200 people under 20 feet of snow. This is the only avalanche in the Himalayas. In 1998 Malpa Landslide disaster occurred in the village Malpa in Pithoragarh of Uttarakhand killing 380 people of the village and pilgrims of Kailash Mansoravar Yatra. 1999 Odisha Cyclone was a super cyclone 05B of deadliest type of tropical cyclone in the Indian ocean Indian storm since 1971. It caused almost deaths of 15000 people and made heavy damages in the areas of Jagatsingpur arasama. In Gujrat a massive earthquake of 7.6 to 7.7 magnitude occurred on 51st Republic day 26.01.2001 in Bachu Taluka of Kutch District killing about 20,000 people. India's heat wave in 2002 at South region most in Andhra killed more than 1000 people. The heat was so intense that birds fell from the sky. The Indian Ocean earthquake and Tsunami occurred in 2004 at the West Cost of Sumatra, killing over 2,30,000 people in fourteen countries, one of the deadliest disasters. In 2007-2008 flood in Bihar was listed as the worst hit flood in the living memory of Bihar which destroyed thousand of human lives apart from livestock and assets worth millions. In 2005, Just after one month of after the June 2005 Gujrat floods, Mumbai the capital city of Maharastra was badly affected and witnessed one of its worst catastrophes in the history of India, killing at least 5000 people. Eastern Indian Storm was severe storm struck parts of eastern Indian states, spanning for 30-40 minutes killing at list 91 people and destroying 91,000 dwelling houses. In 2013 Maharastra State was affected by the region's (worst draught in 40 years) like Jalna, Jalgaon, Dhule areas. Millions of people are affected by famine. Again in the said year 2013,

June Utarakhand received heavy rainfall, massive landslide due to flash floods which killed upto 5000 people apart from damaging millions of houses and structures.

Preventing Disasters

Disasters bring innumerable losses to the society. In order to reduce or mitigate the losses, the approaches will be of rescue, relief, rehabilitation and follow-up are important. This has some key issue to look after. They are like quick and immediate assessment of the destruction and response, quick planning for relief and co-ordinating the factors for relief work and the end quick execution of the plan of action to get the desired target. Prevention activities are designed to provide permanent protection from disasters. Not all disasters, particularly natural disasters can be prevented, but the risk of loss of life and injury can be mitigated with good evacuation plans, environmental planning and design standards. In January 2005, 168 governments (countries) adopted a 10 year global plan for natural disaster risk reduction called the Hyogo Framework. It offers guiding principles, priorities for action, and practical means for achieving disaster resilience for vulnerable communities.

The activities which are designed to minimize loss of life and property are called as the disaster preparedness. For example, it is the removing people and property from a threatened location and by facilitating timely and effective rescue, relief and rehabilitation. Preparedness is the main way of reducing the impact of disasters. Preparedness should be of community based which will help to mitigate the loss of all. The management of preparedness to combat disaster should be of high priority in physical therapy practice management. After preparedness is over, the next work at the front is disaster relief work execution. Disaster relief activities are better if designed in a multiagency method. Relief activities include rescue operations, relocation, providing food and water, preventing and treating diseases, disabled and injured persons, repairing vital services such as telecommunications and transport, providing temporary shelter and emergency health care services.

Disaster Recovery and Conclusion

Once emergent needs have been met and the initial crisis is over, the people affected and the communities that support them are still vulnerable. Recovery activities include rebuilding infrastructure health care and rehabilitation. These should blend with development activities, such as building human resources for health and developing policies and practices to avoid similar situations in future. It requires a well set management process to bring various issues and challenges of disaster into the normal track. Disaster Management is linked with sustainable development particularly in relation to vulnerable people such as those with disabilities, elderly peoples children and other marginalized groups. From the above conceptual and analytical study, it is seen that disasters harm not only to the living being but also to the Nations at large-the Earth. The people inside the Globe must be conscious about the cause of raising these disaster, which are mostly natural and environmental. "The earth is sufficient for the need but not for the Greed". The people are the massive destroyers and so the man-made disasters can be mitigated out of carefulness. Every inhabitant should be alert and conscious while using the earth and in remembering the guiding principle of "Prevention is better than cure". After all if disasters appear fight with full preparedness and with an organized team work and follow-up in order to mitigate the harmfulness of disasters which can't be avoided.

REFERENCES

Source : Health volunteers : overseas publication on disaster management.

World Development Report, 2014.

https//www.fema.gov/disasters/grid/year/2016

disaster declarations, 2016

Google Chrome PPT,

Sambad, 28.12.2004, P-5.

Odisha Review Oct, 2001, Issue

Index